LEVERAGE

TONY JEARY
THE RESULTS GUY™

Clovercroft Publishing

Leverage: A Leader's Answer to Extraordinary Results

© 2014 by Tony Jeary

Published by Clovercroft Publishing, Franklin, Tennessee

Cover Design by Eddie Renz

Interior Layout Design by Suzanne Lawing

Edited by Alice Sullivan and Tawnya Austin

Printed in the United States of America

978-1-940262-51-2

What People Are Saying about Tony and His Work

"His writings are a success 'playbook' that will raise the performance of top leaders across the business world."
—Ricky Richardson, President, TGI Friday's, USA

"Tony is the best strategist I have seen in action . . . He brings energy, focus, and actionable ideas that impact businesses immediately. Engage Tony today if you want to dramatically drive growth in your company."
—Allan Dziwoki, Mitsubishi Electric HVAC

"We are a better organization today as a result of our relationship with you over the last two years."
—Michael Berry, President, Hillwood Properties, A Ross Perot Company

"Tony, you have a truly outstanding Rolodex: you live up to your credo of action, execution, and connecting your network. You always exceed expectations! . . . Much needed content for business—this has the makings of a bestseller!"
—Roman Kikta, Venture Capitalist

"A person's life is richer when they find someone who lives their life on purpose and serves others with their unique gifts—thank you for enriching my life and continually pouring value into others!"
—Ross Lightle, Canadian Business Coach and Mentor

"My relationship with Tony has had a profound impact on my thinking as an executive. His executive coaching and counsel continues to have a positive effect on focusing my team and me on what matters. His principles and methodology provide a powerful tool set to increase employee engagement."
—Peter Galanis, SVP Sales, Equinix

"You are a true Master. We have seen and worked with the best . . . the best investment we have made in years . . . Thank you for coaching!"
—KEITH AND SANDI CUNNINGHAM,
AUTHORS OF *KEYS TO THE VAULT*

"Your library of information, ideas, and systems is a real treasure."
—R. MORRIS SIMS, CORP. VP, NEW YORK LIFE

"My life is better because Tony is in it."
—RON LUSK, SERIAL ENTREPRENEUR

"Thanks for challenging all of us into moving from good to great to Mastery!"
—JOHN WRIGHT, SALES MANAGER, MITSUBISHI

"Tony Jeary is a Master . . . Tony truly does give value and does more than is expected!"
—MIKE ARCANGELO, SANOFI PASTEUR

"I am not only impressed with your coaching skills, but more importantly, your genuine commitment to supporting your clients and building a true partnership."
—TOM GRIMM, FORMER PRESIDENT & CEO, SAM'S CLUB

"I've known Tony for years, and his ability to build great leaders, great thinkers, is extraordinary."
—STEPHEN M.R. COVEY, *NEW YORK TIMES*
BESTSELLING AUTHOR OF *THE SPEED OF TRUST*

"Tony has always been excellent at helping top leaders."
—TONY BINGHAM, PRESIDENT & CEO,
THE AMERICAN SOCIETY FOR TRAINING & DEVELOPMENT

"I have found Tony's insights to be both practical and helpful."
—JAMES O'CONNOR, PRESIDENT, FORD MOTOR CO.

CONTENTS

PART ONE
LAYING THE GROUNDWORK

*"An essential function of leadership is to persuade
and motivate others to pursue excellence by helping
them become willing to exceed expectations."*
-TONY JEARY

The reason this book exists is to serve as a continuation of my life's passion for helping others get extraordinary results by breaking down pre-conceived, self-imposed barriers, thus leading to exponential results in accelerated timeframes.

It is my belief that there's no bigger asset a company has than to get its leaders aligned to a common vision or goal, armed and focused on the right plan of attack that drives efficient and effective execution. This is backed up by decades of proof lived out before me with some of the world's most high-performing leaders and companies.

In the pages that follow, I want to share the culmination of these experiences with you so that you, too, can use leverage to influence the best possible outcomes for your organization, your team, and yourself.

PREFACE

"We are what we do repeatedly."
-ARISTOTLE

In 2009, I authored a best-selling book titled *Strategic Acceleration*. The book (my thirty-seventh title) was the distillation of a quarter-century of experience in working with companies large and small, and observing what made the difference between the high achievers, who produced extraordinary results (organizations and individuals), and those who were unsuccessful or less successful. The difference came down to three words: clarity, focus, and execution.

The biggest takeaways were an ability to gain clarity on their vision and goals (where they were going), focus on identifying what I termed *High Leverage Activities* (HLAs), and then to execute through carefully thought-out and crafted strategic communications. Organizations and individuals able to get this methodology right achieve high-performance, accelerated results. Those that get it wrong can be found struggling or folding altogether. Others, at best, muddle through life and business just getting by, hovering in the "safe" zone.

Now this methodology sounds simple, and it is simple. But it is also hard and takes a very committed level of discipline to maximize efforts. Every week management teams of super-bright highly educated, high-achieving leaders fly to my private studio to build plans based on this simple methodology. The first step is obviously to achieve clarity as to what they as a group really want (to define their vision). You might expect that different members would have different ideas on what their vision and goals should be, but in fact they often have only vague and poorly articulated ideas. They are often managing day-to-day, week-to-week without a clear and well-thought-out plan where all stakeholders win, including the shareholders, the customer, the employees, the part-ners, and the executives.

So, how do you get a clear, well-thought-out-plan focused on results? How do you stay out of the "safe" zone, or worse? How do you do the right things as a leader to create and support a high-performing team?

In the years since *Strategic Acceleration* was published, there has been an overwhelming amount of feedback from clients, audiences, and readers alike about my methodology of *High Leverage Activities,* or what I call HLAs. It is important for us to realize we can't do everything at once, and that time and money are limited and have to be rationed on some basis. In other words, we have to prioritize. Simply put, HLAs are a simple yet powerful way to prioritize. You might call them an "organizing principle."

So how does this all relate to you as a leader? The subject of leader-ship is probably the most written-about subject in business literature. And that is as it should be. A workable business definition of leadership is "organizing a group of people to achieve a common goal." So think of *High Leverage Activities* as an "organizing principle" for leaders to use in achieving the common goal or vision. This book is intended to provide all leaders, top executives, managers, team leads, and even in-dividuals with a practical guide to the art and science (yes, it is both) of using HLAs as a powerful organizing principle to achieve extraordinary results.

From the top, it is about building a culture around the concept of *High Leverage Activities.* At the executive or team level, it is about the simple execution of strategy by focusing limited resources of time, money, and talent to specific goals required by you and your team to achieve the vision. At the individual level, it is about using the HLA concept as an organizing principle for prioritizing the daily to-do list and maximizing limited time. If you are successful at facilitating, leading, and inspir-ing your organization in creating a true HLA-focused culture, then you will win faster. Period. You will grow your brand and reputation. You will also grow your team members while positively impacting financial wins. You will create a win-win-win situation that also roots itself in momentum to continue on the pathway toward your vision. The cas-cading effect from the top down creates habits and behaviors that have an exponential effect on results.

It is important to recognize that the "HLA Principle" is applied differently at the leadership level and the individual level. Both matter a lot. Everyone wants the right results faster! That's what I do—I help people think differently so they get the right results they want faster. And after you read this book, you will be more effective—*I stake my brand on it*. In fact, you will want your entire team to read *Leverage* as soon as possible because HLA thinking is that powerful.

When I ask audiences to define a "High Leverage Activity," the tactically-minded will say something about dousing the hottest fires and killing the fastest alligators. The strategically-minded will talk about doing things that move the needle faster and farther than others. But not all needles are created equally.

If you aren't very clear about what you really want, then you have no guiding principles, no North Star to guide you toward the most important needles you want to move. This book will help you find your North Star, keep that star in focus, and help you think your way through this busy world we live in.

What you really want is to sort out the activities that will move you closer to your goal. In other words, my big secret is to kill the *Low Leverage Activities* (LLAs) that pull energy and other resources from HLAs. Take things off your plate that have no business being there. Your LLAs should be reduced or go away altogether.

Let me give you a military example. You may be able to take a hill quickly and at minimal losses because you have a brigade (thousands of soldiers) and the enemy on the hill has a platoon (less than fifty soldiers). But if the hill is of zero or little strategic value, you have just wasted resources. In fact, you have wasted an entire brigade. That brings us to the "leverage" in the *High Leverage Activity*. Tying up a brigade to overrun a platoon is often anti-leverage. Leverage is when you can use a platoon to take a strategically critical hill defended by a brigade. The pure definition of leverage is to use something to maximum advantage; to have (and exercise) the ability to act or to influence people, events, or decisions. That's powerful.

Now escalate the principle to a commanding general, who is in charge of an entire army. A general who uses his troops sparingly and strategically to minimize the use of resources, while gaining the most important strategic objectives, will have the confidence of his entire army. The army's morale will be higher, as will their confidence in ultimate victory. This wins battles and wars. It can also win in the marketplace. Again, this is evidence of the exponential effect of multi-levels of leadership all working at the highest level of effectiveness.

HLAs require a constant and relentless strategic balancing of resources required against the results envisioned.

Now let me go a little further before we really dig into the book's content. Let's suppose for a moment that yesterday you made a list of HLAs. Chances are that today you need to reexamine that list and make some minor adjustments and changes. When I began my career as a corporate coach decades ago, I could create a list of HLAs and feel pretty sure it wouldn't change much in a year's time because markets evolved at a moderate and manageable pace. A little tweaking from time to time was necessary of course, but building HLAs into a five-year corporate plan was often no problem.

Today, thanks to the world of media and technology, we wake up in a new world every morning. In 2007, the price of oil rose from about $60 per barrel to nearly $100 per barrel in a few months. Few saw the price rise coming and those who did were laughed at. The largest leveraged buyout in U.S. history was the purchase of Dallas-based Energy Future Holding (EFH) for $48 billion. The deal only made sense if one assumed the price of natural gas would remain around $10 per million cubic feet. But almost overnight the price of natural gas plummeted below $2. Now, as of this publishing, EFH is about to become the largest bankruptcy in U.S. history. The very bright, well-informed investors never saw the price plunge coming.

In 2008, the American economy collapsed almost overnight. Again, the very few who saw it coming were laughed at.

Today small events in faraway places can turn our markets upside down. Companies like HP, Google, Amazon, and Apple really don't fear each other, but they do fear the teenager they have never heard of living a few blocks away who will soon invent the "next big thing" and leave them floundering. Chaotic worlds where so-called Black Swan events occur (events that are highly unpredictable that have major impact) with startling regularity require a constant recalibrating of our HLA lists.

The man who popularized the notion of the Black Swan in a book of the same name, Nassim Taleb, wrote on the subject of unpredictability. He wrote another book called *Anti-Fragile* in which he suggested that you cannot manage against something as unlikely as a Black Swan event. So if we can't predict events like these, what do we do? The secret to surviving and thriving in an unpredicted catastrophe is to proactively build your organization to withstand such events.

Even if you take out those isolated, devastating catastrophes, life is moving at warp speed; and the access to technology and information forces constant improvement and innovation to be leaders in your cho sen field.

It is my belief that an HLA focused leadership with an HLA culture in place is the solution to protecting an organization from the negative effects of things that cannot be controlled, while simultaneously building a sustainable competitive advantage.

Getting the HLA list right will result in an efficient allocation of resources, constant measurable progress toward defined goals, and soaring morale because you, your team, and your entire stakeholder community become more confident you are on track to achieving your vision.

Again, this book is about identifying and prioritizing *High Leverage Activities* that drive faster results and achieve a vision that requires doing something most people aren't really equipped or encouraged to do—think.

Several years ago my great friend, former president of my company, and personal coach for more than twenty years, Jim Norman, made the statement that "thinking is hard." My immediate reaction was that Jim was wrong and had made an inaccurate statement. Thinking is second nature to all of us; we think all day long, even when we really don't want to. But Jim wasn't talking about day-dreaming or even typical, automatic responses to everyday activities. He meant the kind of rigorous, disciplined thought process required to analyze complex information and arrive at the best alternative course of action among many options. He meant outside-the-box *strategic* thinking. And do you know what?

Jim was right. That kind of thinking is hard and most of us don't do it well or *think* to do it at all.

When I ask audiences what they need for making decisions, they will answer "information." That's true as far as it goes. Of course you need the right information, and it needs to be timely and accurate; but that's only the beginning.

When I then ask what should be done with the information, the discussion gets fuzzy and tentative. "You have to analyze it," someone might say. "How do you do that?" I ask. At that point the discussion gets a bit uncomfortable. The reason is that most people and most organizations don't have a disciplined thought process. Many don't have a process at all! People simply react based on prejudices stemming from their experiences starting as far back as their childhood. In other words, information is processed through biased filters that may or may not be true.

> IF YOU ARE SUCCESSFUL AT FACILITATING, LEADING, AND INSPIRING YOUR ORGANIZATION IN CREATING A TRUE HLA-FOCUSED CULTURE, THEN YOU WILL WIN FASTER. PERIOD.

In the corporate world, for example, decisions are biased based on our perspective. If we are in finance, we are concerned with things like cost or return on investment. If we actually have to do the work, we often just look on any activity from a functional viewpoint. Others will take a purely political view: Does this enhance my power and prestige or reduce them? Everyone has ego invested in past decisions and will often be reluctant to embrace any reordering of priorities that might render their prior achievement obsolete.

Effective leaders recognize that they and everyone in their organization have these biased filters, and they must work to build a culture intended to overcome these *Blind Spots*. Believe it or not, one of the easiest ways to overcome *Blind Spots* is to consciously be looking for them; and using your HLAs as a filter will go a long way toward uncovering them and will help you see things differently and gain new perspectives. Leadership must constantly question, probe, and improve the status quo. And they should encourage and teach others to do the same.

This book will show you how to balance tactical and strategic thinking and use both to your advantage. If you have the right thought process, if you can weigh evidence and alternatives with rigor, you have a very good chance of identifying and properly prioritizing the HLAs that will drive the results you need—and drive them faster. Bottom line—focusing on *High Leverage Activities* and being open to changing your thinking is the key to success in your personal life and in an organization. It's that simple and that powerful.

> *"The person who says it cannot be done should not
> interrupt the person who is doing it."*
> -CHINESE PROVERB

INTRODUCTION

"Leadership is a results contest."
-Tony Jeary

Have you ever thought about leadership being a results contest? Think for a minute about different times in your life when you've "won" something or been on top of your game. What did that look like and feel like? How were you rewarded differently from those who performed at a level lower than yours?

Results matter in competition, whether it's between individuals or organizations. We all know that all sports are games of inches. A tenth of an inch from the goal is close, but there's no score. The tennis ball hits the line or it doesn't. There's no reward if your ball lands outside that line. No matter how small, results matter; so the effort required in hitting the line or crossing the goal is always necessary.

When I make these kinds of statements in presentations, all heads nod in agreement. Everyone agrees that results do matter, faster is always better, and decimal points count. But while everyone grasps the importance of results, most don't stop to think about the larger picture of a world spinning ever faster and ever more unpredictably. You see, results aren't just about head-to-head competition; they're about staying ahead of the world.

> YOU SEE, RESULTS AREN'T JUST ABOUT HEAD-TO-HEAD COMPETITION; THEY'RE ABOUT STAYING AHEAD OF THE WORLD.

Everybody enjoys winning personally and professionally. This book will help you accomplish both in the fast-paced world we all live in. Invest an hour, and both you as a person and your organization will win more, win better, and win faster. I guarantee it.

The most brilliant business strategy ever conceived will be wasted if it is poorly executed. Just because the strategy is brilliant does not mean results will follow, or that they will follow fast enough. Today, success requires the *right execution for the right results* faster.

Let me amaze you with a few numbers so you can begin to understand what we mean by staying ahead of the world:

- At the outbreak of World War I, 100 years ago this year (2014), the population of the world was at 1.5 billion. Despite the carnage of twentieth-century wars and the terrible flu epidemic of 1918 (50 million died), today the world's population stands at 7 billion and is on its way to 10 billion by the century's end. Yet the birthrate is falling to barely replacement level. How are we still growing?

- The global life expectancy of a human at birth 100 years ago was 31. Today it is 67. Yes, it varies considerably from nation to nation, but these are global averages. Near-daily breakthroughs in medical technology are saving the lives of newborns and extending the lives of the rest of us.

- At the millennium on December 31, 1999, there were an estimated 361 million Internet users worldwide. On New Year's Eve of 2013, there were 2.5 *billion*. These users transfer 638,000 gigabytes of data *per minute*.

- In Asia, there were 114 million Internet connections at the dawn of the century. Today there are over 1 *billion*. There has never been a faster rate of adoption of anything in history.

- In 1999, about 1 percent of all Internet connections were broadband. Today that number stands at 27 percent.

- The first email was sent in 1971; a computer engineer named Ray Tomlinson sent it. Over twenty years would pass before email became generally available to the public. Today, 260 million emails are sent every *minute*.

- In 2006, the iPhone didn't exist. No smart phone did. Today, eight years later, 56 percent of all mobile accounts in the U.S. are smart phones. In South Korea, it's 78 percent. Each minute, worldwide, 47,000 apps are downloaded!

- In 1999, Google was located in a garage in Menlo Park, California. Today Google handles 2 million search queries *per minute.*

- When Ronald Reagan was elected to his second term in 1984 (three decades ago), the world consumed 57 million barrels of oil every day. Today it consumes nearly 97 million barrels. At the time, most experts believed we would consume less today than in 1984. The reason for the change is dramatic new technologies for locating and extracting oil.

- YouTube was created in 2005 when it was located over a Pizza shop in Palo Alto, California. Friends were looking for video of the Indian Ocean tsunami but couldn't find any. Today, 1.3 million videos are viewed every minute on YouTube and 30 hours of video are uploaded to the site *every minute.*

- The visual discovery site Pinterest was launched less than four years ago. In January 2011, it operated from a tiny apartment and had just over 10,000 registered members. Today, just three years later, Pinterest has 70 million members.

- In 1964, a megabyte of memory would have cost you over $2.6 million. Today a megabyte of memory will cost you about 6.5 thousandths of a cent. How's that for technological advancement?

- In 2000, 86 billion photos were taken. In 2014, it is estimated that 880 billion photos will be taken (including a lot of "selfies"). Every year we take 10 percent of the amount of photos ever taken in the history of the earth.

- The amount of data on earth is doubling every 18-24 months, depending on the industry, so Moore's Law holds true: Human knowledge doubles every 13 months.

Yes, we all know the world is changing rapidly. But when I share numbers like these with audiences, it is virtually always an eye-opening exercise of awareness. Very few of us are really aware of just how fast and how dramatically change is occurring. This is the speed of life to-day.

Let's look at this another way: in the world of video games, once you pass one level and go onto the next, the game gets more difficult. For every new level, it gets harder and harder. This translates to business as well. The higher the position, the more difficult the game. Having an effective strategy will better position you to win the game and become more successful.

What this means to you is that we aren't just driving results in a two-dimensional world. All manner of events are occurring that will alter the field you and your organization play on. This means the results contest gets even faster as you struggle to stay ahead of multiple learning curves.

> THERE IS A TSUNAMI RIGHT BEHIND YOU, AND YOU CAN NEVER LET UP.

This is an environment that demands efficiency in the allocation of time, talent, and money. **It means a constant recalibrating of resource allocations. It means reprioritization at the speed of life. It means there is a tsunami right behind you, and you can never let up. It means you have to understand the concept of leverage and apply it at every moment.**

Yes, that may sound terrifying to some. Others are chomping at the bit to ride the tsunami, exceed the competition, and excel in every area of life.

Just by reading this book, it tells me that you care about faster, better, more focused results, and you care about your place in this amazing world.

I encourage you to follow through regarding the teachings within. It may not always be easy, but the results will be your reward for persevering through the transition to leverage.

TAKEAWAYS - PART ONE

PART TWO
THE STARTING POINT

"The journey of a thousand miles starts with but a single step."
-LAO TZU

Every journey has its starting point; and your journey to your vision, organizational or personal, begins with understanding time and leverage, and with clarity of vision. We all have the same amount of time. That is true for every person in every organization. We can only really find more time for one activity by taking it from some other activity. Professionally, time is money. Remember, too, that time is not equal, because some people have superior skills and talent. Either way, time must always be budgeted.

But how do we know how to budget our time? We use an "organizing principle" that assigns a value to time. My belief is that the single-most powerful organizing principle is maximizing leverage by prioritizing action, according to which actions are highly leveraged (produce superior results faster), and which actions are low leverage.

In order to be able to determine leverage, you have to have a North Star to guide you. That constant guide should be a crystal-clear vision of what you want to achieve. This, again, is true both in your personal life and for an organization. You may know where that first step starts; but if you don't know where you are going, you have no hope of ever getting there.

Put the two together: With a constant vision to guide your efforts and the organizational principle of high leverage, you are on the road to success.

CHAPTER 1
TIME AND LEVERAGE

"How an organization leverages time determines its rate of success."
-TONY JEARY

In *Strategic Acceleration* I talked about something called *High Leverage Activities*, or for short, HLAs. In the intervening years audiences and clients have focused on the concept as something deserving of more in-depth treatment. It is fair to say that the HLA concept has proven to be the primary spark for an "aha" moment. The excitement with which management teams and high-achieving leaders have embraced HLAs as an organizing principle for leadership has been deeply gratifying.

Before we talk about HLAs, let's make sure we understand the general concept of leverage. Most of us understand leverage in the physical sense: If you are confronted with a block of granite weighing 1,000 pounds and are asked to lift it, it will be impossible for you to lift it with just your own strength. Even if there were handles on the sides of the block, you simply could not lift the block. On your own, you do not have the strength or size to do it. But if the block is sitting on a very strong and sufficiently long board, and you have a log of sufficient height in the middle of the board, a single person will be able to lift the block by pressing down on the other end of the board. This person doesn't even have to be that strong. This is mechanical leverage. But the same principle can be applied in non-mechanical situations.

Consider financial leverage. You want to buy a company that costs $10 million, but you only have $2 million to invest. What can you do? You can borrow the rest. This means you have only $2 million of your own money at risk (along with your reputation, of course). Now in the past the company has been owner-managed and run as a lifestyle company for two generations. The owners weren't interested in taking risks, just in paying their bills and keeping sales and profits steady for the past five years. You know the industry and believe you can easily cut costs to pay the debt service on the loan without jeopardizing performance. You are confident you can double the value of the company in four years. It turns out you know what you're talking about, and four years later you sell the company for $20 million. You pay the loan (including interest on the original amount), retrieve your original investment, and pocket over $8 million. That's what you call financial leverage.

Let's take a business example that leaders often overlook—"credibility" leverage. The fact is that some people have influence that exceeds their position, so to speak. For whatever reason, people listen to them and take what they say at face value. Whether they are deserving of this trust is beside the point; they have it. If they have a positive outlook on management's plans and goals, they will transmit that outlook to a wide circle. If they are negative, they become a cancer, spreading disbelief and cynicism. If management can identify and win over these people, they have leveraged their outsized influence for the positive. In my expansive involvement in partnering with growing direct selling companies, I've witnessed that credibility can be a significant growth factor, because leaders with credibility breed trust, inspire motivation, and encourage action. I've seen it countless times in the corporate environment as well. This is called credibility leverage.

That brings us to the concept of the *High Leverage Activities*. What tasks will move you toward your goals that are the building blocks of your vision with the resources you have? Resources are always limited. To some degree, all organizations have limited time, money, and talent. **The ultimate plan is figuring out where to put those resources to**

drive the results you need to reach your goals.

Once you have a clear vision, you can begin to set realistic goals. Of course goals aren't something you plant and then wait for them to bloom. Every goal carries a "to do" list required to achieve the goal. To execute each "to do," you probably have a secondary "to do" list—smaller steps required to accomplish the more in-depth steps. In fact the "to do" lists can get pretty long and complex very quickly, even in small organizations.

Envision a wall with 100 gauges. Under each gauge is a knob you can turn to adjust the reading to its desired level. That knob is redirecting a flow of limited resources to the tasks required to move the needle on the gauge. You can turn the knob until the gauge reads 100 percent. The problem is that as you adjust one knob, the flow of energy and resources going to all the other tasks that drive all the other gauges change too. Some change for the better, but some change for the worse.

Now at the top of the wall is one large gauge. Let's call it the "vision gauge." To achieve your vision you must get the pointer pointing strait up to 100 percent. That means that each of the 100 smaller gauges have to be at the right setting (not necessarily 100 percent). The task is possible, because you can look up and see if you are moving closer to or farther away from 100 percent on the vision gauge.

Imagine trying to get this right if there is no vision gauge; it would be nearly impossible or a fluke if it happened. Even with a clear vision gauge, it is still very hard.

In the Rights of Medicine Administration creed for nurses, the mantra is "the right dose of the right drug for the right patient at the right time." The same concept holds true in management. You have to apply the right resources, at the right place, in the right measure, at the right time. But how do you know the answers to these questions? You evaluate their potential leverage.

Goals are not created equally in terms of moving toward your vision. Some get you there quicker than others. Some cannot be achieved until others are achieved first. Action items aren't created equally either. Some move you toward your goals more quickly than others. But if this were simply a race to see which knob could get you to 100 percent the quickest, then prioritization of what to do first wouldn't be that difficult. Again, **you as a leader need to evaluate each task's (or person's) potential leverage.**

As I said, resources are always limited. There is only so much time, energy, money, and talent. Everything simply cannot be done at once. Chances are you can only do a few things at once to do them well. So you set priorities. Which of those gauges can be brought to the desired reading with the minimal amount of available resources? That's what *High Leverage Activities* are all about. You have to weigh the return (movement toward your vision) against the investment of resources required for each. If you could sit in my studio for a few sessions, you would realize just how important setting priorities for resource allocation can be. Weighing the return against the investment will not only maximize your resources, but it will also ensure the maximum return on your time. Time wasted on the wrong things can never be reclaimed.

While there is math involved, this is not just a mathematical exercise. Yes, there are costs to be estimated and budgets to make and Gant charts to be designed. But the numbers can only provide a useful guide. If only numbers were the key indicator, then a properly programmed computer could do a superior job of helping human executives pick the right HLAs. But a computer can't. **Identifying HLAs is about informed judgment, disciplined analytical thinking, and occasionally a gut feeling.**

In a real-life business example of "leverage," consider the efforts of American Airlines to reestablish their customer service levels. The airline had been in financial difficulty since the 9/11 tragedy but was pushed to the brink by the Great Recession of 2008. The company's leadership was hunkered down, trying to find ways to avoid bankruptcy, deal with the increasing expectations from the employee workforce that had previously agreed to pay cuts, and convince Wall Street there was a plan to keep the airline in the air.

For Mark Mitchell, then the head of Customer Experience, it was a challenging time. Mitchell explains, "Our customer research showed clearly that our customers were not as happy with their experience as they were a decade before. It was clear too that our employees were deeply frustrated by the lack of tools and training as service cuts occured. Our employees knew a better American, the one that was an industry leader. For success, we needed more attention from our senior leaders, whose time was spread thin across competing priorities. We knew we had to turn the customer experience into a positive one, but our resources for doing so were very limited."

They were indeed. Mitchell had a team of six Project Leaders to reach out to more than 100,000 employees and dramatically alter the airline's customer interface experience. If ever there were a case where leverage was required, this was one. So Mitchell and his team gathered their research; and in my studio they developed an execution plan for their Customer Blueprint for what an industry-leading customer experience would look and feel like, from both the customer side and the American Airlines employee side.

With their execution plan for the blueprint in hand, the team continued to focus improvement across six basic requirements that could drive the change they needed. One powerful example of leverage came from the identified need to involve senior leaders in the effort. "Given all they had to deal with, that at first seemed impossible," recalls Mitchell. "But we had to show our employee base that this was a high priority for the people in charge. So we asked our senior leaders for just two hours each week where they could visit with our local airport and customer facing teams, hear about their ideas and their accomplishments, and ask questions. This became a great forum for some cheerleading too from our Senior Leaders to those employee teams. It later evolved to being much more centered around our Customer Cup travelling trophy."

Not only were Mitchell and his team of six able to utilize their 170 local teams (feet on the ground) by way of leveraging the two hours a week from each senior leader, they were also able to begin moving a much-needed needle by leveraging an improved customer experience. The result of all this focused effort and the right needle moving? American was able to get through one of the company's most difficult times and thrive. American Airlines serves as a great early example of using leverage in a business situation.

Another key factor in understanding time and leverage for yourself is trusting your direct reports. This allows you to delegate and empower them to help leverage time to get things done. If you cannot leverage down appropriately and trust that things will happen without your involvement, it is likely you will end up spending a disproportionate of your time managing things others should be managing.

Let's now apply the idea of the HLA to your personal life. You only have so much time, and most of us will spend (or should spend) one-third of that time sleeping. Many of us try to cheat the clock by investing longer workdays and fewer hours of sleep. But being capable of a highly productive eight straight hours doesn't mean you are capable of an equally productive twelve straight hours. The fact is, your energy is limited as well. You will likely find your overall productivity declines the longer you work. And you will likely find your health declines too. And no matter how rich you are, you only have so much money and likely have plenty of demands on it already.

Life, too, is like that wall with all the gauges. If you have a life vision, then you have a big gauge in your mind and heart telling you how close you are to achieving it. To get to 100 percent and stay there, you have to keep adjusting and readjusting all of those little knobs called family, friends, colleagues, community, mind, body, spirit, business, and more. And you have to constantly reallocate your time, money, energy, thinking, and love (yes, love) from one task to another to achieve the readings that add up to 100 percent on that big gauge.

This means prioritizing your activities and your time (your most precious commodity) in alignment with your values, according to the highest leverage. Maybe spending more time with your kids will adjust a family gauge that moves all the others in a positive direction and helps keep the big gauge (your vision) pushing 100 percent.

The search for leverage is the critical factor in any results contest, whether it is personal or professional. Understanding just where the point of greatest leverage is to be found and just how to apply it with the amount of time you have to use is challenging. Those who succeed in maximizing time and leverage set themselves up to win, rise above their competition, and gain market share.

VIPs

1. Gaining greater results with fewer resources is utilizing the power of leverage. In life and in business, resources of time, talent, and money are always limited. Leverage those resources and you can go farther faster than you ever thought, using all three for maximum gain.

2. Sometimes leverage is found in the right person, sometimes in the right moment, and sometimes in the right idea that allows you to do more with less.

3. Leverage is an organizing principle for prioritizing your actions and budgeting your resources.

4. Making ongoing adjustments (sometimes small, sometimes big) to ensure your time and efforts support the achievement of your vision is maximizing leverage.

5. Trusting your direct reports, therefore delegating to them and empowering them, will help you leverage your time to get things done.

6. Leverage not only can be used in business situations, but also in everyday life outside of the office, with your family, to achieve happiness and success in all areas of life.

CHAPTER 2
CLARITY

"Complexity is the enemy of everything."
-ANDY STANLEY

Focus is not something that comes naturally; it is a skill that must be developed. But before you can begin developing focus as a skill, you first must be clear on what you need to focus upon. For those of you who have read *Strategic Acceleration*, this chapter will be powerful reinforcement on the importance of clarity and vision from the very beginning. For those who haven't, let me assure you that clarity is the place to start.

So, what is it you really want? What do you want professionally? Personally? For your family? What's your vision for your life? Knowing this is what I mean by clarity.

Let me share the definition of clarity I used in *Strategic Acceleration*. From a leadership perspective, clarity means having an unfettered view of your vision, which is what you want and why you want it, fed by an understanding of its purpose and value. In the old days, executives didn't see any need to explain the why. They simply expected people to fall in line and do what they were told. But when people understand the why of things (the purpose and value), the combination produces a level of clarity that has enough influence or pull to actually become motivational. It becomes the fuel of voluntary change that enables you to be pulled toward your vision, rather than pushed.

Most don't have this definition of clarity and react to a discussion of clarity with reluctance to believe. Surely business and professional people know what their vision is. Yet, every week executive teams come to my private studio in Dallas with only a vague idea of their vision—if that.

Organizations whose executives have a clear vision are easy to find. Each year *Inc.* magazine publishes a list of the 5,000 fastest growing companies in the United States. The list is filled with companies of all sizes working across all industries. One of the most important attributes they have in common is a clear vision of what they want to be and accomplish. I have had the pleasure of helping many of these fastest growing organizations implement these methodologies in the past.

Companies with a complete lack of vision struggle at best; and in worst-case scenarios, they fail altogether.

I've worked with many companies in the direct sales industry, such as Avon and Amway, that allow individual representatives to share their products, and reward them for doing so. Almost every company that does this encourages their new representatives to identify their "why." Why are they choosing to share these products in their spare time? Why do they want to earn some extra income? Why are they willing to make sacrifices to make it all happen? These companies understand the importance of clarifying the "why" with this volunteer army. When people identify their "why"—things like spending more time with their family, getting out of debt, or creating avenues to explore their passions—the ability to say "no" to those things that don't help make their "why" happen becomes so much easier and sustaining. It's a principle that works in any industry, to be honest.

Of course, most companies have some idea of what their vision is, but it is often fuzzy and their management teams are often divided or uncertain. Because of that, their employees and team members are often confused and focus on meager tasks due to lack of clarity of the bigger picture. This often results in lackluster performance and high turnover.

What most executive teams do have are goals. Unfortunately these goals tend to be driven by each team members' personal agendas and politics, placing the goals all over the map without true alignment. For example, the CFO is concerned with cutting costs and risk. The COO is driven by getting the product out the door. The marketing crew wants to drive sales and will push for service improvements, financing options, more product features, or bigger sales teams. The IT contingent will lament they can only do so much so fast. The goals are all ad hoc and don't necessarily contribute to an overriding vision.

The first thing I do in the studio is to get a team to set aside goals and focus on their vision. We can spend half our time on that because it is half the battle. Usually everyone has a slightly different idea of a vision and often they disagree over what a "vision" really is; but over time and with facilitated discussion, they arrive at an "aha" moment with heads nodding in agreement. From that point forward, it is all clear sailing.

> IF THERE IS NOT CLARITY OF VISION, THE BEST THAT CAN BE HOPED FOR IS FAR LESS THAN WHAT IS POSSIBLE.

Let me assure you it is no different for small organizations than large, multi-national corporations. I have worked with many of both and they all have the same issues. If there is no clarity of vision, the best that can be hoped for is far less than what is possible. I don't know about you, but I don't want my efforts day in and day out to be less than what is possible.

It is important to note that **clarity of vision is more than a well-thought-out and written vision statement to go in the company handbook, posted on a website, or tacked on the cafeteria wall. It has to be concrete.**

From a leadership perspective, there must be some basic rules for achieving your vision:

1. The vision must be realistic. It is wonderful to say you want to be number one in your market in two years; but if you have four percent of the market share today, no one will take your vision seriously.

2. You have to have the resources to achieve the vision. This book is about getting far more from existing resources through a particular strategy. But there are limits. Just like a rubber band, if you ask your resources to stretch too far, they can snap.

3. A defined timeframe is also necessary. Saying you want to realize your vision without a timeframe makes progress virtually impossible to measure; and what you cannot measure, you cannot manage.

4. The timeframe has to be meaningful and within reach to the people engaged. Ten-year goals won't inspire anyone, because they are just too far in an uncertain future to be real.

5. What are the benefits of achieving your vision? Your vision also needs to have obvious rewards for everyone who is involved in making it a reality.

Read and reread these five points carefully. You may note that to meet these criteria you also need a very clear evaluation of where you are today. Today you are in the starting gate, ready for the exciting adventure of living and breathing your vision. What are the strengths and weaknesses of your organization? Where do you fall within the spectrum of your competition? What competitive advantages do you have? What is the market's perception of your brand and the value you deliver to customers?

Achieving a unified vision requires much careful thought. Thoughts will help to uncover the strategies required for the vision—one of which is setting goals and allocating resources to achieve those goals. Now goals become relevant. Goals, you see, are the building blocks of vision. When everyone has the same vision, it becomes a North Star to guide goal setting. It is no longer about "me"; it is about achieving "our" vision.

Now the CFO is not just concerned with cost control (always critical); he or she is concerned about how to allocate financial resources to achieve the agreed-upon or newly created vision. The COO is no longer just trying to get a product out the door, but trying to determine what type of methods and processes can achieve the common vision. The marketing team is no longer just focused on moving product, but trying to determine how to achieve the vision. The corporate communications job just got a lot easier, too. They now know what they are communicating to every stakeholder community.

Your vision also provides a rationale for change. It serves as a filter through which all decisions must flow. Let's face it—change is hard and uncomfortable. People seek out comfort and security, and they rarely stray. They will resist leaving their comfort zone with every fiber of their being, unless you give them a compelling reason to change.

If an organization's leadership can provide a common vision, they can justify the results needed as necessary to achieving the vision. Everyone knows the definition of insanity: Doing the same thing over and over while expecting different results. A clear vision justifies different results and that requires change. If your organization buys into your vision, they will buy into the future results and rewards and become truly engaged in creating the change needed to accomplish the vision.

Our client, Alastair Douglas, Director at US Commercial Support – Alcon, recalls that the company was operating in a "quasi separate mode. Each team often worked in a silo to accomplish only its objectives, which often did not feed into the overall vision. When we got clear on the big objective of our company and then evaluated what we were doing to see how aligned we were, a clear vision brought us into alignment. Significant results were accomplished because of that clarity."

Perhaps most importantly, your other leaders and team members will understand they have a reason to go to work beyond just getting a pay check (which they can probably get elsewhere). Now they are part of an effort to create a common vision that makes sense and is energizing. With a clear vision, the water cooler can become a positive place for exchanging ideas and not just for trading rumors. Talent that would never have considered working for your company will now be sending you resumes. Your customers will have greater confidence, too, because they will hear from others that you know what you're doing and are leaders in the market place.

Now let me shift gears for just a moment. **What works for organizations works for individuals, too.** Clarity of vision as we defined earlier—an understanding of what you really want in life—is an absolute prerequisite for success, however you define it. If you as an individual don't know what you really want, you can count on never having it.

Isn't the success of your family unit just as important or more important than your success with the vision in your professional life? I have lived a life by design within my household and it has given me a personal life that some can only dream about. We have a family vision. We set goals together. We spend quality time together. We

> **IF YOU AS AN INDIVIDUAL DON'T KNOW WHAT YOU REALLY WANT, YOU CAN COUNT ON NEVER HAVING IT.**

are aligned. We are clear with each other. We make adjustments when needed.

All of the principals in *Leverage* can be applied to your personal life as well to make sure you are spending the right time on the things that matter most. Remember, exploiting leverage means to use it for maximum advantage. Isn't that what we all want? To get the maximum possible outcome, both personally and professionally?

***

When asked what they really want, many people, maybe most, will answer something along the lines of "financial security." That's not what I mean by a clear vision. Financial security is not achieved by envisioning a money tree. I'm asking, "Who do you want to become, what do you want to experience, and what do you want to share with the world?"

Great artists may become wealthy but they pursued art because they had a clear vision of what they wanted: to create the best art they could. Most of them would prefer to sell their art for lots of money; but their real goal in life was not wealth, but to be an artist.

At some point in your life, there comes a time when you have to develop a clear vision of what you really want, because time to achieve your vision will be running short. Once you have that clear vision, you can begin to set achievable life goals that will become the building blocks of your vision. Without a clear vision, your goals, just like an organization's, become ad hoc and focused on the moment. They will add to nothing.

So our road to success, whether for an organization or an individual, starts with clarity of vision. Without it, you will either fail or muddle through. Why do either when clarity can set you on the road to success?

In the past few years, our client USA Truck increased its stock value 400 percent in only 18 months. Many factors contributed to this amazing run-up; but according to Burton Weis, USA's VP of Human Relations, achieving a clear vision was the launch pad. "In Tony's studio, we get clear. We have become very focused on developing our brand and making sure our choices are aligned with the brand," explains Weis. "We realized that our value add is in the brand and our competitive advantage flows out from that."

With a clear vision, USA Truck's leadership found it could easily communicate its goals to its stakeholders. Everything suddenly fell into place. With a clear and common vision, individual actions produced wanted results because they were being measured against the vision. Leadership found it easier to say "no" because they could refer to the vision and filter out the requests that didn't move the needle toward the vision. It also gave them an easy way to say "yes" without becoming bogged down in politics. "Yes" meant the activity in question was going to move the needle more quickly to the agreed-on vision.

Weis affirmed our methodology: "We have been able to accelerate results at a level that was beyond my personal beliefs. We have reached levels I thought were unattainable." USA Truck's top team visits our studio three to four times a year, and huge wins come of it. This all began when John Simone, CEO, who had worked with us a few years earlier, partnered with us again to "leverage" our experience and best practices in working with many of the world's best and more high-performing organizations to help them get clear on their vision, as well.

People buy vision. It provides a cause, a sense of being a part of something larger than one person. Achieving a vision requires long-term and shorter-term goals, and people need goals. **Vision also provides that all-important North Star against which all actions can be clearly judged.**

VIPs

1. Without a clear vision of where you're going, you can never get there.
2. True clarity of vision provides a North Star to guide an organization's actions and an individual's performance at all levels of activity. All activities can be measured against the ability to achieve the goals that are the building blocks of the vision.
3. A clear vision explains the purpose and the value of the all-important "why," thereby making communication a clear process.
4. Clarity helps remove *Blind Spots* and supports strategic change that leads to results.

TAKEAWAYS - PART TWO

PART THREE
THE ABSOLUTE ANSWER

"No single skill or habit has a more powerful impact on results than the ability to eliminate distractions and focus on High Leverage Activities.*"*
-TONY JEARY

When it comes to getting the results you need to achieve your vision, there is an absolute answer: *High Leverage Activities.* In Part Three, we will explore what HLAs really are.

When you identify HLAs, you are able to focus on action choices that are most likely to advance your vision faster. When a significant portion of time (yours and your organization's) is spent on HLAs, it means you're constantly making the most positive choices, and a winning trend gets established faster.

HLAs are probably the most important aspect of my core *Strategic Acceleration* methodology of clarity, focus, and execution. Execution requires that every person in an organization do what they need to do at the right time with minimum use of time and resources. Even in smaller organizations, execution is challenging. Without a guiding principle in constant use by every individual, politics and brush fires take over. The organization becomes reactive, not proactive. Resources are wasted at every level, and morale sinks as "everyone for himself" becomes the watchword.

I can tell you after working with CEOs of top companies, both large and small, for twenty-five years that this doesn't have to happen. The absolute answer to efficient execution is the HLA.

CHAPTER 3
HLAs ARE THE CORNERSTONE OF EXTRAORDINARY RESULTS

*"If you ever wondered why the Indian rain dance
always works, it is because they dance until it rains!
Simply put, it's focus until completion."*
-TONY JEARY

When you hear the word "cornerstone," what comes to your mind? The cornerstone (or foundation stone) concept is derived from the first stone set in the construction of a masonry foundation. It is the most important stone, since all other stones will be set in reference to this one, thus determining the position of the entire structure. It is key to getting started off on solid footing and to creating a structurally sound building. The most brilliant strategy is of little benefit if it is poorly executed or not executed at all. The best product can be a loser if its marketing strategy is poorly executed. Poor execution results in a massive waste of resources, confusion, low morale, and an overall loss of confidence by stakeholders and customers.

Superior execution means getting things done right the first time, meeting deadlines, exceeding expectations, and conserving resources. It means creating more value at higher levels of efficiency. Superior execution means getting superior results faster.

Yet, in many instances I have found that "execution" is a puzzle leaders struggle to solve. Activity happens every day all around us. People are busy getting things done. But activity doesn't always equal results. Proper execution requires communicating to every member of the organization what they need to do and by what deadline. It means making work product handoffs smoothly and on time. Execution demands interfacing with outside vendors and contractors and customers in a way that allows them to work as an integral part of the overall effort. Superior execution requires a proper allocation of resources to divisions and departments and teams. It requires people who know what they need to do in order to achieve the desired results.

Even for smaller organizations, execution presents a daunting communications, logistics, and budgeting challenge. Many companies have attempted to grapple with execution by implementing large and expensive software solutions for customer relationship management, project management, and a dozen other activities. Dashboards are created that purport to give an up-to-the-minute view of execution reality. Such systems can, in fact, be very useful at providing insight and tracking progress.

But these Enterprise Resource Management (ERM) systems, Customer Relations Management (CRM) systems, and others have a dark side. By and large, people find these systems irritating and resist them. They see them as time consuming and time wasters. Others see these systems as a manifestation of Big Brother watching. Then there is always the old problem of garbage in, garbage out.

From my perspective, these systems are fine when they operate in a culture of execution that has the right organizing principles understood and embraced by the entire enterprise, including involved stakeholders. It is the culture that allows individuals to embrace these systems as tools for success. However, not everyone can afford the latest and greatest cutting-edge ERM systems; yet they can still successfully execute.

The key to successful execution is to embrace and use *High Leverage Activities* as your indispensable organizing principle. HLAs are, in fact, software notwithstanding, the building blocks of successful execution. HLAs provide a principle that empowers a workforce to execute without constant supervision or minute tracking. HLAs are the building blocks for allowing every level of your organization (indeed, every individual) to maximize efficiency and effectiveness, and to utilize minimal resources to achieve maximum results.

In the military they talk about the "fog of war." That refers to the uncertainty in situational awareness experienced by participants in military operations. Generals know that you can draw battle plans in intimate detail; but once the guns begin to fire, plans break down. Unforeseen, maybe unforeseeable, events occur and timetables begin to unravel. Objectives not met by one battalion impact what another battalion can do and when it can do it.

It is not that different when it comes to executing a strategy to achieve your vision. Things go wrong. Deadlines are missed. Handoffs aren't made. Morale ebbs and flows. Resources have to be reallocated. Chaos can result.

The silver bullet for managing the "fog of war" is for each unit and each individual to be trained in the HLA concept where HLAs become the cornerstone of results. It is simply impossible to micromanage complex implementations of strategy. It is the leaders and individuals in the trenches and on the front lines who know best what will move their needles further and faster. They know best what the most efficient uses of resources will be, relative to the results produced. Added together across the board, using the common organizing principle of HLAs, an organization can make amazing headway while minimizing management resources.

In his book *The Effective Executive*, Peter Drucker advises to "focus on opportunities rather than solving problems." It is good advice and fits hand in glove with the concept of the HLA. HLAs tell you where the best opportunities lie. By using leverage, you drive results much faster per resource, especially the resource of time.

To me, the role of an Executive Team is to:

1. Establish the clear vision that aligns all segments of an organization.
2. Develop a well-thought-out strategy for achieving the vision.
3. Set quantifiable goals that are the building blocks of the vision.
4. Communicate and sell the vision and goals to all stakeholders.
5. Allocate resources.
6. Develop a culture built to focus on and execute HLAs.

7. Develop metrics to track the company vision and completion of goals. (Manage the result without hampering performance with micromanagement.)

Consider the role of HLAs in each. An Executive Team that has a grip on the HLA concept will have the confidence to fashion a bold and compelling vision. Knowing that a company uses HLAs as an organizational principle allows the development of a more robust and challenging strategy. Goals can be more aggressive, because the Executive Team knows their organization can execute in the most efficient way possible without micromanagement from the top. Think about that—it's pretty powerful.

Talking in HLAs will give stakeholders confidence that the walk will match or exceed the talk, and that gives them confidence to support the vision. Resources can be best allocated from a bottom-up process with confidence if Executives have confident leaders who understand and practice HLA management.

An HLA culture is a definitive culture that breeds confidence and results. It is not a vague culture of platitudes graphically laid out on a website. It is not a culture where a list of values has no application to the workaday world. It is not a culture of everyone for him or herself.

USING HLAs, YOUR PEOPLE SEE THAT DRIVING RESULTS FOR A VISION IS THE COMMON DENOMINATOR FOR DECISION-MAKING, AND NOT POLITICS OR PERSONALITIES; AND THEY ACCEPT THE NEED FOR COMMON ACTION.

The HLA culture is definitive. It is a philosophy of action and an organizing principle. It has a language that captures a common way of thinking and acting. An HLA culture ties values to action in the work world.

We've discussed what the Executive Team does. Now we'll cover the role of the leader, which is to oversee execution. It is at the leader level that the day-to-day work of actually meeting objectives occurs.

According to Peter Drucker, a leader does five things:

1. Sets objectives for the group or team.
2. Organizes by dividing work into manageable activities and makes assignments of tasks.
3. Motivates and communicates.
4. Measures performance and then interprets performance.
5. Develops people.

Consider how HLAs work across all five points. How do you prioritize multiple objectives? Use the HLA principle: Determine which objectives will get you where you need go the fastest with the most minimal use of resources. How do you determine which tasks will achieve your objective fastest? Use the HLA concept as your organizing principle. HLAs provide a common language for motivation and communication.

Using HLAs also provides clarity for action. Your people see that driving results for a vision is the common denominator for decision-making, and not politics or personalities; and they accept the need for common action. Using HLAs, your people will see rapid progress they probably didn't think possible; nothing is more motivating than seeing success happen.

HLAs give you a common denominator, too, for measuring and evaluating. This, again, gives team members confidence that results matter, results will be rewarded, and results measured will be real.

Finally, nothing helps develop people quicker than a sense of accomplishment. Conversely, nothing is more demoralizing than to feel your time is being wasted or that you are just going through the motions one more day for a paycheck. **HLAs provide a method for individual achievement.** They can see and measure their progress relative to effort expended and know when they are really helping move the needle. It is

> NOTHING IS MORE MOTIVATING THAN SEEING SUCCESS HAPPEN.

so important that every member of an organization goes home at the end of the day knowing and feeling that they made progress and contributed to the goal.

HLAs as an organizing principle becomes the foundation—the cornerstone—of success, because they will always drive the results you need. Put them *Top of Mind* and incorporate other concepts that are a part of the HLA approach, and watch your organization take off.

VIPs

1. Resources of time, money, and talent are limited and must be budgeted. *High Leverage Activities* are an organizing principle for setting priorities.
2. HLAs create a clarity of action.
3. HLAs represent a special language that alters the way you and your team think about what needs to be done.
4. Nothing is more demoralizing than to feel your time is being wasted or that you are just going through the motions one more day for a paycheck. HLAs provide a method for individual achievement.
5. As Peter Drucker says, results don't just happen; the right type of management needs to be in place.

TAKEAWAYS - PART THREE

PART FOUR
YOUR THREE "MUST DOs"

"Success is neither magical nor mysterious. Success is the natural consequence of consistently applying basic fundamentals."
- JIM ROHN

There are three Must Do's for every leader, especially as it relates to HLAs.

First, you have to think more strategically. Thinking is hard. I am not talking about the barely conscience thinking you do when you shop for groceries. I am talking about the disciplined critical thinking required to analyze evidence, evaluate alternatives, and make strategic decisions. In this section we'll discuss how to think and how to focus on what really matters.

The second thing is you must learn to identify your own HLAs and those of your people. Have HLAs for every job description. Learning the power in clear HLAs will become addictive.

The third "must do" is to learn to say "no" more often. Saying "yes" is often easier. For the most part, "yes" makes people happy. "No" often hurts feelings and makes people angry if you say it wrong. Yet, if you don't say "no," your time ceases to be your own and so does your organization. Other people will be making your decisions, because you can't tell them "no." But there is a right way and a wrong way to handle the challenge of "no."

Here I'll show how to use a couple of very powerful concepts that will make identifying HLAs easier to accomplish for both yourself and the people in your organization.

CHAPTER 4
THINK MORE STRATEGICALLY

"Change your thinking, change your results."
-TONY JEARY

Recall the story in the preface about my coach, Jim Norman, telling me "thinking is hard" and my dismissive reaction. After "thinking" on his comment a while, it occurred to me that Jim was right. Thinking is hard.

We think it's easy because most of our thinking is almost subconscious. Each day confronts us with hundreds of simple choices and problems that require thinking—but not too much.

You go to the store to buy a tie and find two you like. One is red and the other is yellow. How do you decide which to buy? You are likely unaware of your thought process. In the blink of an eye, you will mentally inventory your wardrobe, identify the items you are most likely to wear the tie with, recall your wife's likely opinion, recall your current tie collection, consider whether anyone you know has a similar tie, identify your own favorite color, and consider the price. This process isn't entirely subconscious, but it is close. You certainly don't consider it hard to do because it really is second nature.

You get ready to go to work and vaguely recall that there is a road construction detour on the route you usually take, so you decide to take an alternate route that's a bit longer but probably more scenic. Not a lot of hard thinking there either. Again, you are hardly aware of your own thought process.

When you get to the office you get a call from the head of your supply chain who informs you that a crucial shipment of zinc from China will be delayed by several months because their mine has been closed by flooding. There are other suppliers, but they all come with questions. One is price and its effect on the company budget. There are legal considerations, too. This is a complex problem that requires acquiring a lot of information quickly and disciplined critical thinking to evaluate alternatives and their consequences. *This* is the thinking that Jim was talking about, the kind that is very hard.

So what exactly is critical thinking? Consider these four attributes:

- Critical thinking raises vital questions and problems, formulating them clearly and precisely.
- Critical thinking gathers and assesses relevant information, using abstract ideas to interpret information effectively. With these interpretations, you come to well-reasoned conclusions and/or solutions. How do you know if they are well reasoned? Test them against relevant criteria and standards.
- Critical thinking requires you to think open-mindedly and to be willing to change your previous beliefs in order to get new results.
- Critical thinking communicates effectively with others in figuring out solutions to complex problems.

Establishing priorities according to leverage is some of the hardest thinking you will ever do. It's intentional versus subconscious, which is already switching gears. One reason it's so hard is because you know how important the outcome is; the stakes are high and the pressure is on. Most of us don't do our best thinking in stressful situations. (We will dive deeper into this concept later when we discuss "focus.")

Low-stress situations usually occur when there is less at stake. Let's face it; if your new tie doesn't match your favorite suit as you hoped, you can always take it back. If there really was no wreck on the usual route, you lost five minutes. However, misapply resources in more important critical thinking situations, and the consequences can be severe.

When I ask my audiences what the first step to critical strategic thinking is, someone will say something like, "Formulate the problem." That's right; the first step is to clearly define your problem. Almost every business or personal problem you face requires real clarity.

I have coached some of the world's most high-achieving executives. Sometimes people ask me why these moguls would need a coach when they have accomplished as much as they have. Surely they know what they are doing. Yes, they *do* know what they're doing. In fact, they are the very best at what they do. I've had the same coaches for over 20 years, and they continue to give me kernels of wisdom that make me think smarter, get clearer, and make better decisions. Clarity often requires a trained but unbiased eye. It is too easy to mistake a symptom for the illness.

Lagging sales are a symptom of a problem, not the real problem itself. You have to dig to determine whether the cause lies with the product, training, hiring, or some other factor. If you don't have clarity as to the real problem, no amount of thinking will come up with the answer.

Another common response to the first step in critical thinking is, "Gather information." That, too, is correct, but keep this in mind: you need the right information at the right time in its correct and complete form (not a partial picture).

"What next?" I ask. "You need to weigh the information," someone will say. "To see if it is heavy?" I'll quip. There are always a few moans and a few twitters of laughter, but my point is, what does "weigh" mean?

Information isn't created equally. What people attempt to do is first determine just how relevant the information is and then how critical it is. How do they do this? Many do it the same way they choose the tie in the store. They go with a gut reaction based on a virtually subconscious mental inventory in their mind's database of what they believe to be true, based on their experience. Action "A" just sort of "feels right."

That is not the way to consistently drive results. What if our experience was wrong and we didn't know it? More commonly, what if our past learning is no longer relevant today?

Being right requires a lot of subjective evaluation. To do that well, we have to ask ourselves if those mental databases are filled with current accurate information, or whether we are acting on misperceptions, or even illusions. Put another way, do we have *Blind Spots* that cause us to misevaluate information?

Anyone who has heard me give a public presentation in the last few years has seen the FedEx logo that I show on a screen. I ask my audience to find both the hidden serving spoon and arrow in the logo. Everyone in the audience has seen the FedEx logo thousands of times on trucks and boxes and ads; yet very rarely do I have anyone raise his or her hand that has seen both the spoon and the arrow. Usually several moments pass before someone sees them; sometimes no one sees them at all. Everyone in the audience begins to really understand *Blind Spots*. We all, in fact, have *Blind Spots*.

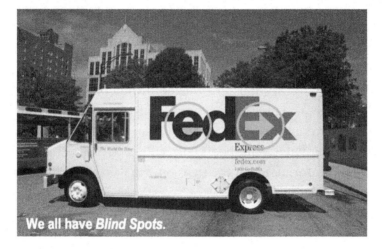

We all have *Blind Spots*.

The same can be true of our people judgment. One bad encounter or even one bad report from a source we don't really know can poison our opinion of someone we barely know. We mark that person off our list of people we want to work with or entrust projects to. Yet that person may be the only one in our organization with the background and skills to execute a critical project, and we rejected the person based on a false impression. Unfortunately people are stubborn about their opinions. Rather than seeing if our impression might be wrong, we stick with what we think we know and turn a critical project over to another who doesn't even come close to getting the results the other person would have achieved.

Critical thinking requires a constant updating of our mental database. Let me give you an example (chances are you know this story, and it will just be a reminder) of a false belief based on a childhood experience carried forward thirty years.

I once attended a seminar about false prejudice. The moderator told a story about how a lady fixed a roast by cutting the ends off. One day a friend asked why she was cutting off and throwing away perfectly good (and expensive) meat. The lady, caught off guard, coolly told her friend that she did so because that was the way you fixed a roast.

Later, she realized her defensiveness was misplaced. She prepared the roast that way because her mother had. But why, she wondered, did her mother cut the ends off? She called her mom and asked why, and was told that was the way her grandmother prepared roast and to call Nana for the reason. When she did, her grandmother was incredulous. "It was the depression and that was the only pot I had; and the roast wouldn't fit, so I cut the ends off and cooked them separately," she laughed. "Surely you aren't still using that old pot!"

This is an amusing but excellent example (most have known for years) of how past information can be misunderstood with the passage of time.

Here's a recent example of a more important nature. A man was approached by the CFO of a large corporation to take on a "supply chain transparency" project. The object of the project was to actually visit the facilities of tier-one suppliers and appraise them for safety, environmental quality, worker treatment, and a range of other factors. The CFO also wanted to know about tier-two and tier-three suppliers. Given that the corporation had over 6,000 tier-one suppliers, this was obviously an expensive and time-consuming job.

Then there was the bigger question: What if serious problems were found? Would the corporation demand reimbursement or actually change suppliers if a problem was discovered? Such changes could be costly, indeed.

The company's CEO was opposed to the idea. Part of the reason was the cost. But the greater reason was a doctrine generally enforced among many large corporations: plausible deniability. If a foreign factory was using forced child labor in a firetrap, the corporation flat-out didn't want to know about it. The CEO wanted it to be someone else's problem, not his. Besides, he reasoned, who would really know, since the factory was thousands of miles away in a third-world nation?

The much younger CFO had a different mental database, based on different experiences. He understood in today's world of social media, that any event could be instantly communicated to a billion people within minutes. He also understood that a corporation's greatest asset today is its reputation, and that a reputation built over decades of honest dealings could be destroyed in a day. The CFO understood that it didn't matter whether the company could plausibly deny knowledge of wrongdoing; they would take a serious hit to their most valuable asset— their reputation. From a risk management point of view, the CFO understood that the project would be money well invested; not to mention being the right thing to do.

The younger executive could cite dozens of examples to make his point. The CEO hadn't heard any of these examples before; he had not updated his mental database. He was still acting from outdated experiences. All he wanted was the right product at the right price, delivered on time.

Our world transforms itself daily. We all know it doesn't take long for knowledge to become outdated, for skills to weaken, or for paradigms to shift. It is true that some things, like basic values, never change. But a lot of knowledge comes with a "sell by" date, and serious thinking requires that we constantly check that date.

The world is filled with stories of corporations that failed because they couldn't change their thinking to meet new conditions. Consider the American icon Kodak. Eastman Kodak invented the digital camera. Yet, it was the digital camera that destroyed the company. Why didn't Kodak own the digital imaging space? Because their executives considered themselves a "film" company and believed that moving to digital technology would put them out of business. Of course what really happened was that too many executives feared the devil they didn't know, so they opted to let others put them out of business. They missed the boat as a huge consequence.

Or consider Blockbuster, the massive nationwide retail chain that rented movies for home viewing. Blockbuster no longer exists. They were laid low by Netflix, an upstart that rented movies through the mail for a set monthly fee. The fact is that Blockbuster, at one point long before Netflix came along, considered the very same service. But they decided not to because the new business model didn't allow for late fees, and Blockbuster garnered a substantial percentage of their income from late fees (which their customers hated). Executives simply couldn't see how they could survive without the late fees. Netflix saw how you could not only survive, but prosper. The old paradigm was destroyed by the new paradigm.

Old thinking that doesn't shift with the times has unnecessarily destroyed millions of jobs and untold stockholder value. Unless you are willing and able to, as Abraham Lincoln once said, "think anew and act anew," you are likely to make very poor choices regarding your vision and your plans to achieve it.

A key job of an Executive Coach is to help clients find their *Blind Spots*. The best CEOs in the world are just like you and me—they have *Blind Spots* and outdated information. A big part of my job is to help clients identify and overcome *Blind Spots* and to be sure their mental database is up to date.

Communicating is also a key factor in critical thinking. Can you effectively communicate your thought process to others? Can you listen to their feedback with an open mind? When you identify a problem and develop a solution, you need to be able to effectively communicate the thought process that led you to the problem and then the solution; otherwise the very people who have to execute your solution may be doubtful and unmotivated.

If we are liable to make mistakes based on false premises, we are also in danger of making mistakes based on false expectations. When Executive Teams have their "aha" moment and a shared vision emerges, the room is filled with excitement. A breakthrough has occurred, and they know it. Long-delayed and much-needed progress has occurred, and the future appears attainable. I have seen battle-hardened, no-nonsense executives become positively giddy at such moments.

But there is a danger lurking. Now that a clear vision has emerged, it seems almost impossible that the vision won't be achieved. In part, that is a good thing. You can't achieve what you can't visualize; and their clarity of vision provides the necessary positive attitude. But this euphoria can also lead to thinking the future difficulties will be easy ones and unpleasant realities don't need to be monitored. Organizations do not live by vision alone and neither do individuals. Anything worth doing will not be easy. A clear reading of reality is still necessary, and thinking requires a strong dose of reality.

Throughout every organization and every team are people who think about solving problems the same way they think about buying a tie. They think in a rut. Worse, they think defensively. **When an organization develops a unique HLA culture, individuals begin to change their thinking patterns to real disciplined critical thinking . . . with intentionality and purpose, aligned with goals, and with an open-mindedness to change previous thinking.** This is when futures are forever changed.

VIPs

1. Thinking can be hard.
2. Establishing priorities according to leverage is some of the hardest thinking you will ever do. It's intentional versus subconscious.
3. Critical thinking is about raising vital questions and gathering and assessing relevant information to see the whole picture more clearly.
4. Critical thinking requires a willingness to expose your *Blind Spots* and change your mind about what you previously believed.
5. To put critical thinking into action, request effective communication with others, not only in figuring out solutions to complex problems, but also in the execution of the solution.

CHAPTER 5
IDENTIFY ALL HLAs
(YOURS AND YOUR PEOPLE'S)

"We don't miss what we haven't imagined."
-TONY JEARY

We have discussed that the amount of "leverage" offered by a specific activity varies. *High Leverage Activities* get you the results you need faster *with less expenditure of time, money, energy, and talent.* Conversely, *Low Leverage Activities* (LLAs) consume resources and drive results more slowly. Identifying HLAs are simply a powerful organizing principle for prioritizing your to-do lists. As our client Rob Budd, VP of Mid Atlantic Sales at Delta Dental, puts it, "Since I have been using the HLA principle, I have a much better sense of what's activity and what's productivity."

But powerful doesn't necessarily mean easy. You have to be able to identify what activities have high leverage and which ones don't. That entails an ability to estimate the resources required to execute a task, and the likely results to be obtained in a measureable time frame.

It also requires an ability to measure the "value" of the necessary resources; or, as Rob Budd puts it, "HLAs provide a much better sense of what takes up time but yields minimal results." For example, a little bit of a lawyer's time may be a questionable resource if the hourly charge is $800 an hour. But a lot of the lawyer's time may be a relatively cheap resource if the charge is $200 per hour.

We have also touched on the elegant but super powerful concept of MOLO: More of/Less of. Determining what you need more of and less of to reach your goals often has a big impact on identifying the LLAs from which you may need to redirect resources.

Here is another important point: It isn't just about the big picture. The big picture is created by the actions of many individuals who must identify the HLAs that will move their section of the enterprise. Unless everyone does his or her part, there will be slippage and it will be apparent. However, when people see the needle moving forward, they become inspired and begin to act as a real team. When they see or feel the needle standing still or slipping backward, they lose confidence in the vision, the strategy, and the goals. They may begin to send out their resumes for another job—maybe even with one of your competitors.

Alastair Douglas, the client we mentioned who is a Director at US Commercial Support – Alcon, uses "value" as the measure for the company's HLA identification. "Using HLAs, we are able to see how a lot of our activity was not really that good for adding value, so we either outsourced those activities or just quit doing them." When everyone in your organization thinks in terms of what activities add the most value, it is amazing to see the amount of progress that can be made in a very short period of time.

***

In various rulings, the United States Supreme Court has held that a corporation has the rights and responsibilities of a singular person. By this they mean that a corporation stands before the law as you and I would. Of course, a business is not a person. It has no brain and does not think in and of itself. It has no morals or sense of right or wrong. A corporation is really a bundle of contracts creating mutual rights and responsibilities among its executives, employees, associates, vendors, customers, and other stakeholders.

The thinking is done by the Board, CEO, other C-level executives, senior leaders, and so forth down the line, truly encompassing everyone. The moral and ethical values of the corporation are a reflection of the moral and ethical standards of the company's leadership, but also arise from the overall standards of the entire workforce. A corporation's success or failure is the cumulative effect of the actions of the people.

To influence these actions, management creates systems, methods, and processes (or repeatable steps) used to get things done. The goal is to develop these repeatable steps to represent the most efficient way to do work. Management also attempts to create a "culture" around a common vision and shared values, intended to encourage specific outcomes. Most companies are more successful in the mechanical area of methods and processes than they are in defining and creating a true culture. Methods and processes more easily lend themselves to measurement, and therefore produce hard data. Culture is difficult to measure, and therefore harder to justify at budget time—or evaluation time.

I bring these things up because when we talk about an organization identifying its *High Leverage Activities*, I cannot overemphasize that it is individuals at all levels of the enterprise that really make the identification and take the steps necessary to achieve an HLA. For an organization to make progress toward its vision, its individuals, starting at the top, must agree on the vision, establish the goals, and then begin to identify the HLAs that can achieve those goals. But let's be clear: the concept must "cascade" down and through the enterprise. This is how you create a High Leverage Culture.

In Chapter 7 I will provide a roadmap for creating this HLA culture. Right now, let's discuss how to identify an HLA with the understanding that we are talking about an individual process that reflects into the larger body.

MOLO

Let's go back for a moment and apply the concept of MOLO (More of/Less of) to a corporate example. Remember, the idea is to determine what you need "more of" to achieve the goals that build your vision. Sometimes you are making an affirmative statement that you need less of something because you know that something is eating resources to no purpose (like excessive meetings). But often you discover that you need less of one thing because, to get more of another, you have to redirect finite resources. Life (and business) is full of tradeoffs.

For example, let's say your vision requires that you take significant market share over the next two years. At present your product isn't the cheapest, but it is competitively priced; and you have found that while price is always an issue, it is rarely the determining factor in buying decisions for your product (this is evidenced in Apple products, where they continue to be leaders in the industry when they are also consistently priced higher than other technology brand products). When it comes to product features, you rule the roost. However, research has found the real determining factor is "service." Customers want a short instillation cycle, rare downtime, and a very fast service cycle. Unfortunately, you are probably the worst among your competitors at providing service.

Note that low market share isn't the problem. It is a symptom. The question is: What are the problems behind the symptom? The research says (a) you take too long to install your product; (b) it is frequently improperly installed and expensive trips are required to fix issues that should never have occurred; and (c) the product is buggy and requires frequent service. Above all, you are noted for delivering service with a frown.

This is your company's brand as others see it—a solid product with many useful features offered at a reasonable and competitive price, but with truly awful service. It is clear from your research that if you can rebrand as the "service company" that "gets it right and keeps it going" you can begin to gain market share. You also know you don't have a long time to get this done. Starting in less than a year, many of your largest existing contracts will be coming up for renewal and your VP of Sales has said several are in danger.

At the same time, many large contracts held by your competitors will be coming up for renewal. So your future is rife with peril and opportunity. If you can achieve your service transformation, you have a shot at holding the most existing business and gaining significant market share.

Clearly what the market wants more of is "service." But achieving faster and better service results and building buzz about your achievement will require more and better communication that makes an impact on your clients. You want your customers to know about your goals, you want them to become partners with you in helping design your enhanced service system, and you want them to know when these goals are achieved.

You will also need to communicate this goal to your stockholders, and that's going to be a challenge. For decades you have paid a generous dividend through thick and thin. In fact, your stock doesn't really move much because it is a dividend play. But to obtain the necessary funds to build your new service paradigm, you are going to have to trim that dividend. You are also going to have to admit that your current model is broken. This may cause some shareholders to sell and depress the stock price. Only if the stockholders agree with the longer-term vision and the plan to achieve it are they likely to stick around. That requires more and better communication.

Unfortunately, the needed transformation funds cannot be found solely in the dividend account. There is a point below which it would be foolish to cut. That means resources will have to be shifted from activities elsewhere in the company. That means *more* "cost control and cost reduction" elsewhere. Immediately every person is on guard. They know cuts are coming and that some of those cuts will be in head count, and the response to most cost-control requests will be "no." Again, you are going to need more and better strategic communication to sell the vision to people who will not see the payoff for a couple of years—if ever.

So the strategic imperative of achieving high service ratings has created a cascade of other "more of" and "less of" measures that involve every person in the organization.

If this is true for the organization, it is also true for every individual at the company. Just because human resources are cut back doesn't mean individuals are allowed to produce less. In fact, their workload will increase. There will be a lot of new hiring in service and new training, too. There will also be terminations. The new service paradigm may also require some changes in HR's methods and processes. Yet, there will be no money in the budget for new software or new hires in that department. HR is being challenged to do more things differently with fewer resources.

The results are that all HR employees now have to think differently about their job. They have to reevaluate their job in the light of new goals and determine what they personally need "more of" to do the job, and what they can use "less of," as resources of time and money will shrink.

What many senior executives forget is that organizational transformations aren't just a new budget and a revised organizational chart. Real live people who come to work every day must make those numbers a reality. And that requires that all individuals think for themselves as to how to reorder their workday using MOLOs to achieve the personal goals that will add to achieving the department's goals, and so forth, until the company's vision has become a reality. Without the personal initiative of MOLO thinking, the vision will remain a mirage.

Note that all MOLO activities don't require major shifts like those mentioned above. Oftentimes, significant results can be had by shifting the focus in small, consistent ways to consciously and intentionally spend a more appropriate balance of your time on those activities that have the biggest impact to achieving desired outcomes.

Because we live in a world that moves so fast and changes daily—maybe even hourly—we often get mired down in just driving through tasks to completion—activity versus productivity, as previously stated. Think about your own situation—what is on your plate that you should be spending less time on, and what is on your plate that you should be spending more time on? If you did this, what would be the bottom-line impact? Now, multiply that impact by every person on your team, and you should be excited about the opportunities that are already right before you. What can you do tomorrow to move toward a shift?

TOM

The next requirement for developing a sustainable HLA list is called TOM, which is short for *Top of Mind*. This concept can be used to identify HLAs but is also indispensable in their execution.

First, let's quickly consider *Top of Mind* as a tool for identifying HLAs. Ask yourself, "What do I think about most of the time?" It's a variation of the problems that keep you up at night. However, what you think about can be more positive. If there is a particular opportunity that consumes your thinking, then that is a clue that the topic may be an HLA. If your vision requires a dramatic increase in sales and you have been thinking about where sales opportunities are geographically or demographically located, then opening new territories may be a key HLA.

If you have been thinking about your CFO and how difficult it is to work with that person or get the answers you need in a timely and understandable manner, then you may need less of that CFO. In fact, you may need no more of that CFO at all. Replacing the CFO with a more positive, faster-acting, and clearer-minded individual may, in fact, be an HLA that can move the entire enterprise forward at little cost.

Now let's consider the *Top of Mind* concept as it applies to the individual. One of the most difficult challenges individuals face when they determine to make a significant behavioral change is sustaining the change. You can say to yourself, "That's my last cigarette," and sustain that behavior for a few hours, maybe even a day or two; but the craving to go back to your old habit gets stronger and stronger, until finally you cave in while rationalizing "just this once."

Or there is the familiar "work out" resolution. You spend the time from Thanksgiving Day to New Year's Day stuffing yourself and then you resolve on January 2 to head to the gym and shed those extra inches. But well before Valentine's Day, your old habits have reclaimed you and the waistline is permanently expanded.

When individuals decide to make a change in their personal life or their professional life, they create new priorities and new habits while shedding old ones. The HLA-focused individual must develop an HLA way of thinking and acting. This isn't the norm. Most of us simply develop habits that continue throughout our lives, even if they cease to get the job done at some point.

If individuals go to work every day for twenty years doing the same jobs the same way, it is hard for them to suddenly change everything. But if they understand and accept the vision and the need for change, and are dedicated to making the adjustments needed, they can get there if they understand how. In fact, somewhat to their surprise, they can be totally energized by the new challenge. They begin to think about the changes needed and begin to talk to their fellow team members all the time about them. Their jobs are fun again.

But change is hard. Over time, minor irritations turn up. The negative attitudes of the disaffected begin to infect us. The day just doesn't seem long enough. The brush fires seem endless. So people begin to let up. The old ways and habits are easier, so they crowd out the new ways and impede the development of new habits. At first, it's just a one-time exception, but then the exceptions become the rule; and soon all enthusiasm for transformation is lost and old habits prevail.

What has happened here is that the *High Leverage Activities* needed to transform their daily activities have ceased to be *Top of Mind*. Like the New Year's resolution to shed a few pounds, the HLA fades and finally disappears altogether. If every person succumbs to this malady then the corporate vision will be lost. The essential element for success in an HLA organization is that every team member personally and individually keeps his or her own HLA list *Top of Mind*.

So how does someone overcome human nature to resist change and stick with old habits? How does one keep the new ways *Top of Mind*? One answer is "Intentional Congruence."

INTENTIONAL CONGRUENCE

Intentional Congruence is a strategic concept that helps individuals develop the habit of focusing on HLAs and sustaining that focus over as long a period of time as is required to transform their thinking, actions, and habits. The simplest definition for this is to **do everything you do on purpose**—but it isn't that simple.

True *Intentional Congruence* comes from our core beliefs about values and is the foundation of everything we believe to be true or false. We always make choices consistent with what we believe. If we believe our fellow humans are always out to cheat us, we will react with mistrust and paranoia to anything anyone tells us. If we believe people are out for themselves and lack any concern for others, we will react accordingly by being self-focused and deceitful. If we believe everyone shades the truth, then we will have no guilt about shading the truth as well.

In our example, if individuals are cynics whose life experiences have led them to believe all corporate decisions are made to fatten C-level wallets, then they will be resistant to any requests for change on their part. However, if they have seen corporate transformations work and believe that corporate leaders are interested in building value, they will more willingly accept and engage in change.

Do people really know their values? Yes, they know them vaguely. But most people don't really take the time to sit down and list them out. They don't really know what their most basic beliefs and attitudes are or where they come from. **Taking the time to sit down and make such a list can be a real eye-opener for most people (see TJI Values Card Decks in the bookstore at tonyjeary.com).** They will discover the source of destructive attitudes and even the existence of negative attitudes they didn't realize they had. It will allow them to see how these attitudes cross all areas of their lives. Those who believe it is okay to shade the truth at work will find they shade the truth at home.

> DO PEOPLE REALLY KNOW THEIR VALUES? YES, THEY KNOW THEM VAGUELY. BUT MOST PEOPLE DON'T REALLY TAKE THE TIME TO SIT DOWN AND LIST THEM OUT.

The importance is to compare the HLA list with the basic values. If they aren't congruent, they won't work. It is that simple. Something will have to give. If an HLA and your values are compatible, then you will be able to keep the HLA *Top of Mind* and drive through to complete the goals the HLA is intended to achieve.

Why is this issue of HLA/Values congruency so important? In my book *Strategic Acceleration,* a significant portion deals with something I call *Strategic Presence. Strategic Presence* is your personal brand—the way you are perceived by the world. A positive strategic presence is produced by the congruence of what you believe you are, what you say you are, and the things you do.

Robb Budd knows how hard Delta Dental worked to assure their HLAs were congruent with their value proposition. "Because we have complete alignment between the HLAs and our values, we are very aware of selling value that connects with our sales prospects as well as the broker we work with. Our having 'value' out front in our thinking leads to a competitive advantage for us."

Another interesting example comes from Roman Kikta, who runs Mobility Ventures, an early-stage investment firm focused on wireless communications. His organization's core value is the entrepreneur. Roman explains, "The idea has to make sense and have a market, but lots of companies with good ideas fail. The difference maker is the passion of the person who had that idea and his or her willingness to make the sacrifices and take the risks needed for success." For Roman's company, HLAs are about supporting the entrepreneur. "How do we help that person who has bet his or her life savings on an idea to succeed?"

Some investment firms would look to replace the entrepreneur as quickly as possible with a seasoned executive. But Kikta and his partner value the passion of the entrepreneur. The Mobility Ventures brand stands out as "valuing" the entrepreneur. Now if you are someone with a bright idea who's willing to risk it all, who would you want as your investment partner?

Let's use my own personal brand as an example. If I did not really do all the things I advise others to do, my personal brand would have no credibility. Everything I say others should do, I do! When people come to my *Strategic Acceleration* Studio and I talk to them about the importance of goals, I can show them all of my goals in writing. Not only are they in writing, but I post them visually as a reminder of my journey.

The same is true for everything I say and do. How is this possible? It's only possible because my values and my actions are compatible and congruent. The result is the credibility of my personal and professional brand. Put another way, my positive *Strategic Presence* is produced by the congruence of what I believe I am, what I say I am, and the things I do.

The congruency of my brand is one of the most important things that I have made *Top of Mind* in my life. I think about it constantly, and I am always asking myself if what I am doing is consistent with my values. What naturally flows from this is a constant thought process about my HLAs. *My Intentional Congruency* is a key strategic accelerator in

Tony Jeary's Results/Vision Board

my life. My HLAs are the action part of that puzzle. Therefore, HLAs naturally become *Top of Mind,* and it is easy to keep them there.

If you want to know more about *Strategic Presence* and why it is so important, check out my *Strategic Acceleration* book. And remember: When you are in tune with your values and you know the values you live by, you become intentional about every aspect of your life. *Intentional Congruence* produces *Top of Mind* awareness.

In my case, my personal brand and my company brand are the same thing. The company is identified with me. My values are the company values. I hire people based to a great extent on whether their personal values are similar to mine. In some cases, I turn down new client opportunities based on a conflict of values. I have no interest in sullying my reputation through association, no matter how big the check.

I frequently meet with teams whose members have conflicting basic values. I am not talking about disagreements over whether to focus on service or sales or over opening a new sales territory in another country. Those are valid points of argument. I am talking about basic matters of telling the truth, serving a larger community, or taking care of individual team members. A team divided along these lines will rarely agree on a vision; and if they do for expediency's sake, they will never achieve it.

In a corporate enterprise, it is more complicated. As we have discussed, corporations aren't people. There is no central brain or consciousness. There is, however, a type of collective brain and consciousness. It is the ghost in the machine. It is called culture. Culture is about organizational values; and, like the "vision," it becomes a measuring stick for all activities. You hire people because they have the right skills but you should also hire them because they have personal values congruent with your organizational values.

Southwest Airlines has a unique corporate culture. It requires a unique personality and a set of personal values that are congruent with that of the airline. To be a part of Southwest, you need to know how to have fun. Candidly, you need to be a bit quirky. Southwest developed a unique interview process that involved asking prospective hires to tell their favorite joke. Interviewees were also given situations drawn from the airline's experience and asked how they would handle the situation.

A friend of mine was once stranded in Austin as a thick fog rolled in. The last flight of the day was in jeopardy of being cancelled; and the lone ticket agent, a young woman named Rosie, was besieged by angry, impatient people. My friend said the crowd had grown so demanding that he was thinking about calling airport security. But to his amazement, Rosie kept smiling, telling jokes, and expressing empathy while keeping everyone apprised of the situation over the intercom. Most of all, my friend was impressed with how Rosie leveraged all these things to get the job done. Soon the crowd had calmed down and moved on. What seemed to be a major problem was solved.

The next day my friend wrote then Southwest CEO Herb Kelleher a letter telling him about Rosie's amazing performance. A month or so later on a Southwest flight, he picked up their in-flight magazine and found Rosie had been named employee of the month and singled out as epitomizing the Southwest attitude. Clearly Southwest Airlines knows how to create an HLA-filled culture. The work of a single employee faced with a very difficult and volatile situation had an enormous impact on that entire company.

Now let's put the theory aside and let me show you a powerful exercise I invented that we use with many of our clients that helps identify top-level HLAs. I call it a *Stakeholder Matrix* (see illustration on p. 78). There are four columns. In the first column we create a list of stakeholders. In the second column, add their DISC personality style if available. It will be helpful in determining the best ways to communicate with them. In the third column we identify what the stakeholder can do to help achieve mutual goals. Column four is a list of high-level HLAs.

Divide your list in half. The first half consists of outside stakeholders, like the end customer, middlemen such as retailers or professionals, or associations. What is your stakeholder's expectation that you have to exceed? That's your value. Most of the middlemen will want growth and profit, but some may also want influence, wins to tout to their members, or happy clients.

The second half of the matrix consists of internal stakeholders. Stockholders, executives, direct reports, and internal support groups are all part of this stakeholder group. What do stockholders want? They want their capital increased by ever greater multiples. What do the executives want? Growth, solid risk management, positive exposure, ease of reporting, clarity, and wins are some of their goals.

What actions can they take to help achieve the vision? The answers are your HLAs. If your customer demands a value your product doesn't provide, fixing the product is your number-one HLA. If the customer loves the product but can't warm to your packaging, that becomes a top-tier HLA. If your customer tells you they love your product but can't figure out how to assemble it, you should be redrafting your instructions as a top HLA.

If you have major retailers for your product like Costco or Walmart, you will want them to communicate your message through their shelf talkers, promotions, and sales and pricing. Anything you can do to support your retail partners is an HLA. If you have an association partner of many thousands of professionals positioned to educate and influence your end customer, then supporting them is likely a high-level HLA.

STAKEHOLDERS MATRIX

#	Stakeholder	DISC	What They Want	What They Can Do
	Owners			
1.	Shareholders			
2.	Board			
3.	Chairman			
4.				
5.				
	Executive Management			
6.	CEO			
7.	President			
8.	EVP Sales / CSO			
9.	EVP Marketing/ CMO			
10.	EVP HR			
11.	EVP Operations/COO			
12.	VP IT / CIO			
13.				
14.				
	Member/Associates			
15.				
16.				
17.				
	Strategic Partners			
18.				
19.				
20.				
	Customers			
21.				
22.				
23.				
	Influencers I.e. Promoters, Rainmakers, Media			
24.				
25.				
26.				

Over the years I have developed about a dozen proprietary matrix-type tools that help organizations identify HLAs and help divisions within companies or even teams identify their own HLAs. We will look at some of the best ones in future chapters.

VIPs

1. *High Leverage Activities* are driven by organization-wide vision and goals, but it is the individual at every level that has to embrace the organizing principle of the HLA and implement it.

2. It starts with MOLO: More of or less of. What do you need more of to get where you want to go, and what can you do with less of to get there? Sometimes the "less of" can be more important. If you are spending vast amounts of time on the wrong things, you are wasting that time. Only when you recognize that those time-sucking activities produce very little can you begin to refocus on what will move your needle.

3. When looking to identify the *High Leverage Activity*, be sure you have reached the heart of the matter, which is to say, don't mistake the symptom for the illness. Always look for the why behind the why.

4. What do you think about most of the time? Put another way, what is *Top of Mind*? That is usually a pretty good guide to where you should be putting your activity.

5. We are all creatures of habit. Some habits are good and some are bad. But as circumstances change, many good habits, or at least harmless habits, can become bad and you have to identify and break them. HLAs are a powerful way to break bad habits. They identify the change required to meet goals and achieve a vision and become motivational for behavioral change.

6. *Intentional Congruence* between values and HLAs breeds a high level of confidence in an organization that is doing things right.

CHAPTER 6
LEARN TO SAY
"NO" MORE OFTEN

"Be willing to say 'no' to good things so
you can say 'yes' to extraordinary things."
-TONY JEARY

Arguably, the most powerful word in any language is "no." It is certainly the most unpopular. And it is also one of the most difficult for us to say. No one wants to say something that others don't want to hear or that will create an uncomfortable situation.

But here's what I know: The word "no" is one of the most empowering words in your vocabulary. While it's often associated with a negative response, it actually has the power to open some of the most positive experiences of your life. Learning when and how to say "no" is one of the most valuable lessons of leadership. Handling "no" the wrong way can cause disastrous consequences. Handling "no" the right way can become a strategic habit. Gaining leverage in your life starts with focus. Focus starts with the word "no." As you take your first steps toward incorporating *High Leverage Activities* into your everyday life, it's foundational that you establish a clear understanding of the positive power of this little word.

"No" is usually used when someone asks you to do something you don't want to do. We often use "no" when we think the request is foolish or bad: "Mom, may I have the car keys tonight?" Response: "No." The result: a teenager stomping down the hall and the sound of a door being slammed.

Even though the result isn't pleasant, you know "no" is the right answer. Much good is accomplished, and they'll get over it. It is still hard to say, because we don't want the hassle of an angry teenager; and, well, we know how we felt in their shoes.

Consider a more difficult example from professional life. One of your brighter, harder working, but more insecure team members comes to you with a less-than-solid idea that they've clearly spent a lot of time thinking about. They are very proud of their idea and clearly have an emotional investment in it.

> HANDLED INCORRECTLY, A "NO" CAN CAUSE DISASTROUS CONSEQUENCES. HANDLED PROPERLY, A "NO" CAN BECOME A STRATEGIC HABIT.

You consider the idea but your gut is waving a red flag. Your experience tells you it just won't work. But, concerned that you may have a *Blind Spot* that keeps you from seeing the benefits, you seek additional input. Steadily the objections mount. The right answer is "no." That doesn't make it any easier to say, because you know the team member will take it badly and you don't want to discourage that person from bringing you innovative thinking in the future. How you say "no" now becomes paramount. But the importance of saying it still exists.

The fact is that people ask you to do things because it is most often to their benefit for you to do the task, and saying "no" can create havoc in their jobs, direction, or even their lives. How many times have you said "yes" when you knew it was the wrong answer, simply because you knew one day you would need to ask your co-worker for assistance and knew the answer would be "no" out of spite?

Another problem with saying "no" is our natural desire to be liked. "No" does not win popularity contests. It sometimes makes other's lives more difficult. It positions us potentially as someone not willing to help, which is not typically the case. At no time is this more the case than when a family member, friend, or co-worker calls up to chat when you have an important deadline pending. Who wants to irritate a spouse by telling him or her you don't have time to talk about dinner plans? Who wants to brush off a son or daughter who wants to tell you about the afternoon's athletic triumph? Clearly, what these people want to talk about can wait, but being put off with a "no" is never well received. They get a message that what is important to them is not as important to you as something else.

Why all this time spent on "no?" Because "no" is the key to focus, and focus is the key to tackling *High Leverage Activities* successfully; and regularly completed HLAs are the key to achieving the right results faster. I also wanted to put all the reasons out on the table why we typically say "no" so we can eliminate the excuses and learn to reframe our thinking.

It could be argued that saying "no" should be a part of every leader's job description. Given the demands on a leader's time, learning to say "no" is the only way decision-makers can possibly control their time to focus on the right activities. Teaching others throughout the organization the power of "no" should be a high priority for anyone in leadership. Empowering your people (no matter where they are, or how big your team or organization is) to say "no" also creates a realization among them that "no" is often the right answer, and they should not be offended when they hear it. It also develops an understanding that everyone's time is not created equally in a business situation. That's not meant to be egotistical; it is just the truth. If as a leader

> "NO" IS THE KEY TO FOCUS, AND FOCUS IS THE KEY TO TACKLING *HIGH LEVERAGE ACTIVITIES* SUCCESSFULLY; AND REGULARLY COMPLETED HLAS ARE THE KEY TO ACHIEVING THE RIGHT RESULTS FASTER.

you are spending time doing administrative tasks, then every minute spent on those tasks is taking you away from an HLA that brings a much higher value and return to the company.

In my office, I have a set of performance standards, and the very first one says, "Save Tony's Time." This requires me saying "no" often. Even if it takes my team members ten times longer to do something than it takes me, by their doing it, we have leveraged my time, which has an exponential return to our bottom line. It also frees up my mental space to continue to bring innovative ideas and value back to our clients.

Most of us start our days with "to-dos" fixed in our mind, and likely captured in our phone or notebook. That is our agenda for any given day. We know the mental and physical steps required to execute each to-do. We plan our day around making those steps happen, allotting time and arranging schedules accordingly. We know at the day's end we need to have thick red lines drawn through every item on the list to stay on pace to move our needle.

Then it starts.

If you work at an office, you're certainly no stranger to the "quick question" that can easily last 20 minutes and has more to do with your visitor finishing a cup of coffee while recapping his or her weekend to you than anything truly work-related. Then it's a phone call from a colleague that, while important, has nothing to do with your looming to-do list. Just as you hang up, you see a last-minute can't-miss meeting invite from the boss that manages to take up your next 90 minutes. By now, you're nearing lunch time, and you've done nothing to address that to-do list you started the day with.

On another day, the guy whose job seems to be wandering about with his coffee mug telling everyone about his daughter making the cheerleading squad shows up at your door to brag (or he calls to give you an update). Experience says this will be a ten-minute interruption. After he moves down the hall, and just as you begin to get into your first item, your cell phone rings. It's your neighbor. This will be another ten minutes. Finally you get started half an hour into the day, but an hour after that your boss calls with a snap meeting. This time you can't say "no." The meeting lasts an hour and half. Now it is lunchtime.

And these are just a very few of the distractions we all deal with.

So goes the afternoon—people calling with requests or questions; the steady ding of email arriving; text messages from everyone. It takes time to remember where you left off and recover your train of thought. Suddenly it is five o'clock, and you can hardly draw a single red line on your list. Your day is gone.

The power to controlling your day lies with learning to say "no."

For some people, it is difficult to find the balance between being focused and being responsive. After all, in today's workplace…and in life . . . we are multi-taskers whether we want to be or not. With the current state of technology and the pace with which the world moves forward, this is a necessity. Or, another way to put it is driving parallel progress. This is important, but it must be done strategically; and it is critical to continually be conscious about the things you should stop doing in order to maximum your efforts and value.

> ### THE POWER OF CONTROLLING YOUR DAY LIES WITH LEARNING TO SAY "NO."

What most of us have to do is develop "focus" as a skill. Actually, focus is a "strategic" skill because of its enormous leverage. When you learn how to really focus on a task at hand, you will drive results faster and you will win bigger. Results are the ultimate accomplishment for implementing this strategic imperative.

How do you learn to focus? Let's first consider distractions. Specifically, let's start with those distractions that we create on our own. The first person we must learn to say "no" to is ourself. These are the activities we would prefer to engage in other than what we have determined we really need to do. Even if these activities are beneficial overall, if they are done at the wrong time they create distractions from progress and results.

Maybe it's reading *USA Today*. I love to read this paper. I always find useful information but rarely information I need right at that moment. It can wait if it needs to, and I have to tell myself "no."

Most people like to complain about their volume of email. Yet most people are addicted to email. We reflexively check our email ten or more times a day. Then we can't bring ourselves to delay responding to each email, even when they can clearly wait. Most of our inbox can wait and should be dealt with in a prioritized matter. (See my book *We've Got to Start Meeting and Emailing Like This.*)

Now let's talk about saying "no" to others.

This is typically the hard part. Distractions from others often come in very legitimate forms. Let's examine different types of ways that others get you to vary from your planned agenda.

Perhaps you've been at the company the longest, so people automatically come to you for answers. Sometimes you have team members lacking confidence in making decisions they are already empowered to make, so they want confirmation before moving ahead. Other times, individuals may want to give you updates or ask for updates on projects you are working on. On a personal level, people just want to touch base and say a quick hello. Still others may need information from you in order to finish a project or a deadline.

We've identified many of the obstacles; now let's talk solutions.

Part of successfully saying "no" is that it becomes a part of the culture, so it is an expected and even respected part of the internal communication. It isn't about the word itself, but about the intent behind it. The sole intent is to free yourself up to better prioritize your time—time that the company has expectations of and has placed a premium because you're a leader.

I recommend talking with your team and discussing as a group the premium on every person's time. Discuss that every person's time is not equal in terms of dollar value. Everyone's time is important and should be considered accordingly. But as part of efforts to change thinking and be open-minded to ways to be more efficient and effective, saying "no" may be an appropriate response. Also note that sometimes saying "no" really means saying "not now." That could include items you may group for specific times instead of ongoing throughout the day. It may mean you need to defer a meeting or a conversation until you've finished with other priorities.

Establishing the "no" as a part of a positive culture and establishing a commitment to becoming a more high-performing team can often create a positive challenge versus something of dread. And, bottom-line, it can be extremely freeing when you can say "no" without your team members having to feel guilty or worrying about damaging relationships.

Use other people or things when possible to help you with your commitment to your focus on HLAs. Use your administrative assistant, if you have one, as a gatekeeper when you need time blocks without distractions. If your office has a door, take opportunities to close it and perhaps put a note on the front saying something like, "Thank you for respecting my focus at this time – I look forward to connecting back with you after _____." In the blank, offer up a better day or time you would be available. If it is an urgent item, let them know to interrupt, of course.

For those of you without an office, a headset is often a way to tune out distractions. At my office, I prefer to have a more open concept that has many benefits for my team. However, this can create some inherent distractions. I often walk through to find multiple people using headsets to help them focus on their current priorities, and it works well as an alternative to the distractions.

Chances are you can't spend eight straight hours buried in your to-do list, so schedule a couple of breaks during the day to return calls, answer email, or walk to another office to follow-up on an important conversation. Just be sure not to get derailed for the day.

Where all of this leads to is the need for improved structure and habits. You need to have discipline and leverage systems every day. Know and avoid time killers. If you know filling the coffee cup likely costs you ten minutes, then you need to schedule two trips per day and not use an empty coffee cup as a subconscious excuse to kill time six times a day. You also need to be very aware of habits that consume time. People are creatures of habit who rarely realize a habit when they see one.

Follow these steps, and you can filter out much of the distracting noise of everyday life and remove from your reach many of the temptations you allow to distract you from the job at hand. You will be amazed at how much uninterrupted time you can claim back.

There is still the challenge of saying "no." One of the most critical things anyone in leadership has to learn is when to say "no" and how to say "no."

One of my most simple and powerful rules (see my book with Peter Thomas *Business Ground Rules*) is to say "yes" to what you want more of, and say "no" to what you want less of. Obviously, "yes" needs to be said throughout the organization in order for things to get executed. The main point is to change your mindset about automatically doing things you've already done that may not be HLAs. Saying "not" to the right things will mean saying "yes" to more things that matter and that can have the biggest impact.

Learning to say "no" more will give you flexibility, time for yourself, and more control over your time.

If you want more time with your family, learn to say "no" to activities that crowd them out and "yes" to more requests from your spouse and kids (or parents, for that matter) for family time. If you want additional income, say "yes" to activities that have the chance of driving more income and "no" to another fishing trip with your buddies. If you don't believe your spiritual life is what it should be, say "yes" to Sunday morning at church and "no" to sleeping in. If you want to get that contract finished, say "no" to anything that will distract you from writing it.

Learning when and how to say "no" is a priceless skill. Without it you cannot effectively focus; and if you can't focus, you are not going to get very far in using the High Leverage methodology. And my experience tells me that the more time spent daily, weekly, monthly, and annually in your HLAs will yield dramatic results in your success. Learning to say "no" to what you want less of, breaking time-consuming and non-productive habits, blocking distractions, and bringing structure to your day will set the stage for driving the results you need faster.

VIPs

1. Learning when and how to say "no" is a critical attribute of leadership. Leaders keep their organizations and people on course by saying "no" to distractions or *Low Leverage Activities*. Done properly, people will understand that you are saying "no" because their request doesn't fit into your strategic priorities.

2. A clear guide to determining when to say "no" is the Rule of MOLO or More of/Less of. Figure out what you need more of. To make the time to get more, figure out what you want less of. That's what you discipline yourself to say "no" to.

3. "No" is the key to focus, and focus is the key to tackling HLAs; and HLAs are the key to achieving the right results faster.

4. Making the power of "no" an accepted and respected part of your culture should be a high priority for anyone in leadership.

5. Learning to say "no" can be the most freeing and empowering gift you give yourself for gaining control over your life, both personally and professionally.

TAKEAWAYS - PART FOUR

_____

_____

_____

_____

_____

_____

_____

_____

_____

_____

_____

_____

_____

_____

_____

_____

_____

_____

_____

_____

PART FIVE
YOUR ORGANIZATIONAL SUCCESS

"Take time to document what really makes you
successful and strategically aligned."
-TONY JEARY

Organizational success is built on an HLA Culture. That means that everyone from the CEO outward, within and throughout the organization, understands the meaning of leverage, the power of the HLA, and how to identify HLAs.

An HLA culture is about clarity of vision, attainable goals, and always thinking in terms of what can move the needle farther and faster, relative to the expenditure of time. An HLA culture has its own language. People in an HLA culture not only think in terms of HLAs, they use the language of HLAs. Leverage is always *Top of Mind* and guided by a clear vision.

Translating the various concepts we have discussed into practical day-to-day action is the focus of the next three chapters. We will talk about how to create an HLA culture. I'll provide a practical guide for the leader on how to implement HLA thinking and action at the team level, and then tackle how HLAs are used by all individuals from the CEO outward in executing their everyday tasks.

Dozens of my clients have created and executed organization-wide campaigns to establish an HLA culture. They have found the methodology invigorating. Their results show up again and again in their value/

stock price as their organizations act with clarity and purpose.

Leadership is the indispensable factor for creating an HLA culture. Leadership must walk the walk, and not just preach sermons. If employees know that the company leadership is truly dedicated to its vision and embraces and embodies the values it espouses, then the organization will reflect those actions in its culture.

CHAPTER 7
BUILDING AN HLA CULTURE

"No single skill or habit has a more powerful impact on results than the ability to eliminate distractions and focus on High Leverage Activities."
-TONY JEARY

Corporate culture can be a lot like an iceberg: the part above water that can be seen is the only part to which attention is given. But it is often what is below the surface that, being left alone, creates surprises, dysfunction, and even disaster. I don't have to remind you of the *Titanic*. All of your culture, good or bad, will define you; and not paying attention to it doesn't make it go away. Being intentional about your culture and having open communications about the methods and processes used within will create multi-wins. Acknowledging and rewarding those who embrace the culture change is a great way to make it stick.

Oftentimes even leaders who accept the benefit and the necessity of developing the right organizational culture put it off to spend time and money on what they perceive as more urgent needs. But, truth be told, many just don't know how to create or change a culture and aren't all that certain as to what type of culture they want.

My belief is that corporate culture is not only real; it is one of the most powerful factors in organizational success. The wrong culture means failure, while the right culture means success. I also believe that the culture that "just happens" without it being intentional usually happens for the worse. If you want a culture that drives the right results faster, you have to create it, nurture it, and constantly invest in it. You have to be deliberate about it. So I want to take a few pages to talk about what culture is and isn't and show you why it matters. Then we can talk about how organizational leaders can create a desired culture, even when an existing culture is unproductive or even poisonous.

What is culture? Culture is the characteristics of a particular group of people, defined by everything from language, religion, cuisine, social habits, music, and arts. It is a word for people's "way of life" or the way a group does things. There are often cross cultures within a culture. These are sometimes compatible and sometimes they are not.

For instance, my wife and I chose to send our girls to a private Christian school for their education. We made this choice because of the culture it provided that would reinforce the values and beliefs that we espoused as a family. There are many religious denominations represented within the school walls; however, each family has made a choice for their own reasons concerning major qualities and components of the school that have value for them and their individual decision to be a part of that environment and culture. For us, while everything is not necessarily done the way we would have it done, we believe the overall commitment of the school is to grow, teach, and prepare their students for a positive future.

But surely "culture" means something different at the company level. Let's look at the major components of a successful organizational culture and how diversity fits within the culture.

ORGANIZATIONAL CORPORATE CULTURES FOCUS ON:

1. **Clarity of Vision.** *An organization's members have to understand and accept a common vision of what the group is going to achieve.*

Notice I say, "accept." We've defined vision in previous chapters, so we won't dwell on that here; but people have to believe your vision is attainable, consistent with shared values, worth achieving, and that it will be of benefit to them personally. In other words, we are talking about more than a vision statement in the company handbook. We are talking about your guiding star. The ability to move toward the vision is the standard against which all objective programs and projects are measured.

2. **Values.** *The dictionary defines "values" as the relative worth, merit, or importance of something.*

These are not things that should go without saying, like "honesty." A corporate value might be "innovation." That isn't necessarily the no-brainer it would seem to be. To some companies, "tradition" and "risk aversion" may be more critical and positive values than innovation. The CEO of an airline once told me that a company transporting thousands of people a day in a metal tube hurtling through space at 600 mph and then bringing them to the ground in a controlled crash needed to permeate every nook and cranny with a risk-aversion culture.

Or consider Texas Instruments. Texas Instruments has always prided itself on a culture of precision-engineered innovation. Engineering in and of itself was a value. So was innovation. To TI's engineers, design was irrelevant, even a waste of money. So for decades TI manufactured the finest digital watch in the world. It was also the ugliest watch in the world. But no one knew much about it either way, because it was sold with the office supplies and calculators, not jewelry. TI's corporate culture didn't value design, and it didn't occur to them that it could matter to the consumer.

Apple has great engineers and values too, but Steve Jobs "valued" design above all else. Design was part and parcel of the Apple culture. It permeated everything from the workplace to the product. Apple's products are elegant and delightful. The respective cultures of TI and Apple have played a crucial role in their success over the years. Apple enjoys arguably the most respected brand in their space, and yet they are also consistently the most expensive. They know their customer, know what they want, and are unapologetic about asking more for their preferred product.

3. **Behavior.** *How does your team interact with each other and in critical relationships outside the company?*

Some companies build a culture of respect. They want their employees to understand the importance of each job in the company so they will develop an overall culture of mutual respect. This internal culture of respect will spill over into the larger marketplace. Some companies prefer a competitive culture where employees are expected to fight over bonuses and other perks.

Many investment banking firms are built on hyper-competitive cultures that have little respect for anyone who doesn't come in as number one.

Walmart has engaged us for years, beginning way back in the 90s. And one of the most powerful parts of their culture is their daily meeting. They take this meeting seriously and with extreme discipline...all over the world, in every store, in every country. I remember coaching the president of Walmart Japan years back and even observing their daily meeting. At their meetings, they gathered around a table with no chairs. That's right, no chairs. They had the meeting on the entire day in 10 minutes. This behavior around the world is ingrained into their culture—brief, powerful meetings to set the course for the day have contributed to their successful operation for decades.

4. **Accomplishment**. *Put simply, this means consistently exceeding the expectations of every stakeholder at every level.*

Exceeding expectations is key in today's world, but many companies have a culture of just meeting expectations. Put another way, they are willing to just get by and hope their everyday low prices will float their boat. Sometimes that will work; but today, not often. If your company can't meet your stakeholder's expectations you're out of the game—competition and what your customers have to say about you in this virtually connected world will crush you. Every interaction with your company needs to trigger delight.

I have a friend who bought his wife an iPhone shortly after the first one came out. She told him not to, as she was perfectly happy with the flip-phone she had. He got it anyway. At first she was annoyed. But when she powered up, he told me you could see the "delight" in her face. It was a magic moment. Today, she buys only Apple products. That is true accomplishment.

5. **Language.** *This doesn't mean the language of everyday communications. It means the key words that shape thinking.*

Hamed Shahbazi, Chairman and founder of TIO Networks of Canada, a bill payment solution provider, has worked hard to develop and spread an HLA culture throughout the company ranks for several years now. He has an interesting take on what an HLA culture means. "The language of clarity, focus, and execution, along with the organizing principle of *High Leverage Activities*, has given our company a common language."

He notes that "When you first hear the HLA concept, you say, 'Well, of course,' but then you realize you never do it. Building an HLA culture means getting all of your people to think in terms of words like clarity, focus, and leverage. We constantly ask if we are leveraging our resources to the highest level; we never asked that before."

Hamid doesn't think it is a coincidence that the development of an HLA culture and its language has led to the tripling of TIO's stock price.

To summarize, an organizational culture is built on a shared and accepted vision, mutual and widely accepted values, behavioral norms, and accepted levels of accomplishment.

Creating an overall culture supporting HLAs and encompassing all of the attributes above is important for maximizing efforts across the board. Joanne Moretti, former VP of Sales Excellence and Dean of the HP Sales University, understood this. Not only did she support the HLA culture with her own team, she also made HLAs a cornerstone of her leadership development and included my *Strategic Acceleration* process into her leadership development classes designed to build "legendary leaders" within the company. Joanne has a passion for mentorship and built a world-class university for which she attained significant recognition. She was awarded Best New Corporate University of the Year in 2011 for her outstanding efforts in building HP University. (Joanne has now moved on and is building a world-class sales excellence program at Jabil, a global design, manufacturing and supply chain solutions firm.)

Hopefully, this single story makes clear the reality and the importance of culture. Now what I want to do is show you how to build a corporate culture around the idea of the *High Leverage Activity*. Done right, it will address and develop all four key factors in corporate culture: vision, values, behavior, and accomplishment. Language will be incorporated into each key factor.

First let's consider vision in the context of an organizational culture. As you and your team develop your vision, ask yourself:

- Is it realistic to achieve in the given timeframe?
- Do you believe in the vision, or is this an exercise in necessity?
- Is the vision inspirational in a way that will motivate?
- If you do believe in it, can you sell it as attainable to your executive team, employees, investors, vendors, and customers?
- What are the values the company needs to embrace and embody to achieve the vision?
- What are the behavioral norms you need to establish to achieve your vision?
- Can your company embrace a culture of accomplishment that lends itself to always exceeding expectations?
- Do you personally have the leadership skills needed to achieve your vision, and if you need to make personal adjustments, are you willing to do so?
- Do you speak the right language, resulting in the right behavior in your everyday tasks, from strategic planning to sales to customer service?

VISION AND RESULTS BOARDING

Let's assume you have the right vision. This vision is what you are going to build your culture around, so there is really no more important job for the top executive than selling the vision. How exactly do you communicate that vision in a way that gains acceptance?

Walk out into the lobby of your corporate offices and find a blank wall. That is about to become your "vision wall." It is a wall where, in text and graphics, you will provide a storyboard of your company's vision. Visualization is a powerful tool for both an organization and an individual. I have a vision wall. It surely changes over time, but all my goals and all my family's goals are found on that board. We check it often. I ask myself and others if I am meeting the goals required to achieve the vision. (Go to YouTube and search for "Tony Jeary Results Boarding" for a powerful must-watch three-minute video.)

It is absolutely no different for a company or any organization, although maybe a bit more challenging to capture graphically. But it can be done. And it will serve as a daily reminder for every employee and every visitor to your office. Or, how about creating a screen saver of your vision board for your team?

Delta Dental is an example of a company that has incorporated the Vision Boarding concept to great effect. "Delta Dental has embraced Tony's concept of using Vision Boards in our sales efforts," says Rob Budd. "We use HLAs in conjunction with Vision Boards to ensure that we are spending our time on things that matter. We keep the Vision Boards in several locations in our offices for all to see." Budd notes that the Vision Boards help keep priorities in front of employees and ensure that everyone leverages their time. "On our Vision Boards we have the logos of every company we are pursuing mounted there."

The next step is to create a "Results" Board for every department, division, and team next to the Vision Board. Each of these groups needs to know the company vision, and they also need to know the specific goals their group needs to achieve to make the vision a reality. They also need to know the accomplishments or results they will have to achieve to meet the goals. Obviously the Results Board is dynamic. It has to capture movement toward goals and reflect the results accomplished.

What you are doing is creating a visual representation of your roadmap to your vision. It provides a quick and easy picture of where you are on that road at any point in

Customized Vision/Results Board

time. It reminds you of progress, and progress breeds confidence and high morale. The Vision Board and the Results Boards frame a big-picture reality that every stakeholder needs to see to understand the combined organizational effort.

The creation of a Results Board for each sector of the company also allows individual teams to understand where they are at any point in time on the road to success. The Results Board also allows the sub-teams or groups within the larger groups to understand their broader role in achieving success. It is easy to forget that everyone wants to know his or her job matters. It is also easy to overlook the fact that each part of a company needs to understand the importance of what every other part is doing toward the overall success. Understanding breeds respect, cooperation, and collaboration. As simple as it seems, the Vision and Results Boards can create this broad understanding.

So isn't it about time you create Vision and Results Boards for your company and encourage your departments to do the same?

VALUES

At first blush, the idea of company "values" seems a bit silly. Companies don't have values; people have values. Companies have values only to the extent that senior management says they do. So why go through an exercise to create such values? Here are four:

- **Your values inform company policies.** If your values say that your people are your most valuable asset, it is more likely that policies across the board will be those that attract and retain the best.
- **Your values inform decision-making**. Every day every team member makes choices. If the company has clear values, they have a signpost to guide that decision-making.
- **Your values shape relationships.** If mutual respect and open communication are values, then you will build a culture where all stakeholders are treated with respect. You will build a culture where people can and will collaborate toward mutual goals.
- **Your values set standards.** What are your performance standards? Is it okay to just "get by" and do the minimal amount possible? That's what you get with the wrong values. With the right ones, you get a constant effort to exceed expectations in all areas of endeavor.

Ask yourself: What are the core values our company must subscribe to in order to achieve an HLA culture? As mentioned earlier, there are some values like "honesty" that should go without saying. What about "innovation" as a value? Some companies need this as a core value because they must be in a state of constant innovation to compete. For others it may not be relevant.

Each year the United States Department of Commerce awards the Baldrige Award to companies that achieve the highest standards of "quality." Is quality a value or a goal or both? It depends. Some companies sell products into a marketplace that doesn't demand or even want quality in its products. The demand is for the lowest possible cost. For other products in other markets, quality is the beginning and the end. Price is a secondary issue.

What about individual contributors? What do your company values say about your view of your human capital? For years I have heard executives tout their workforce as being composed of the "best in the business." But frequently their policies didn't confirm that. Their companies were inflexible, unreasonable, and indifferent toward individuals. As a result, they had high turnover and low productivity. So ask yourself, "Are the values our company claims as its foundation ones that will attract and keep the right kind of individuals engaged long-term?"

Many executives tell me that the customer is at the center of their world. "Listening" to customers is a core value. But they don't walk their walk. The listening stops as soon as the customer tells them something they don't want to hear. There was an IBM TV ad a few years ago that showed a legion of faceless people moving zombie-like toward a business executive in his dream. The faceless mob was his customers. All too often that is exactly how business sees their customers—as the enemy. There is a crisis of "values" here.

"Values" are not a throwaway for the company handbook or website. They need serious thought. Your values truly reflect what you want from your extended company and how you intend to achieve your vision. They have to be right for your aspirations, your vision, your industry, and your company. They have to make sense. They also have to be taken seriously.

IT STARTS WITH AUTHENTIC LEADERSHIP

You cannot have "open communications" as a value if a company's leadership refuses to engage in open communications. Others will not do what the leadership refuses to do. If you are unwilling or unable to walk the walk, either the values or you need to change.

You cannot tout employee-friendly values if the top executives are abusive. That doesn't mean you cannot succeed with values that demand performance above all else. Ross Perot's EDS succeeded brilliantly. Steve Jobs was notorious for mistreating his top people, but top people beat down the door to work for him. Apple's culture was not built on cuddly values, but it still succeeded.

It is worth taking a look at the stated values of Apple:

Apple Values are the qualities, customs, standards, and principles that the company believes will help it and its employees succeed. They are the basis for what we do and how we do it. Taken together, they identify Apple as a unique company.

These are the values that govern our business conduct:

Empathy for Customers/Users

We offer superior products that fill real needs and provide lasting value. We deal fairly with competitors and meet customers and vendors more than halfway. We are genuinely interested in solving customer problems, and we will not compromise our ethics or integrity in the name of profit.

Aggressiveness/Achievement

We set aggressive goals and drive ourselves hard to achieve them. We recognize that this is a unique time, when our products will change the way people work and live. It is an adventure, and we are in it together.

Positive Social Contribution

We build products that extend human capability, freeing people from drudgery and helping them achieve more than they could alone. But beyond that, we expect to make this world a better place to live. As a corporate citizen, we wish to be an economic, intellectual, and social asset in communities where we operate.

Innovation/Vision

We built our company on innovation, providing products that were new and needed. We accept the risks inherent in following our vision, and work to develop leadership products that command the profit margins we strive for.

Individual Performance

We expect individual commitment and performance above the standard for our industry. Only thus will we make the profits that permit us to seek our other corporate objectives. Each employee can and must make a difference. In the final analysis, individuals determine the character and strength of Apple.

Team Spirit

Teamwork is essential to Apple's success, for the job is too big to be done by one person. Individuals are encouraged to interact with all levels of management, sharing ideas and suggestions to improve Apple's effectiveness and quality of life. It takes all of us to win. We support each other and share the victories and rewards together. We are enthusiastic about what we do.

Quality/Excellence

We care about what we do. We build into Apple products a level of quality, performance, and value that will earn the respect and loyalty of our customers. At Apple, quality management is critical to our continued success.

Individual Reward

We recognize each person's contribution to Apple's success, and we share the financial rewards that flow from high performance. We recognize also that rewards must be psychological as well as financial, and we strive for an atmosphere where each individual can share the adventure and excitement of working at Apple.

Good Management

The attitudes and behaviors of managers toward their people are of primary importance. Employees should be able to trust the motives and integrity of their supervisors. It is the responsibility of management to create a productive environment where Apple Values flourish.

What are the words that stand out? To me they are: empathy, aggressiveness, achievement, innovation, performance, quality, risks, reward, and team. These values say Apple is an action-oriented company that expects to wake up to a new world each day and expects to master that world. It is willing to take serious risks to do so and will reward those who are aggressive, innovative, take risks, and perform. Overall Apple's values indicate a tough and demanding but exciting place to work that offers substantial rewards for those who fit in their culture and perform.

Apple spends a lot of time explaining why these values are Apple's values and what they should mean in the practical terms of performance, policies, relationships, standards, and decision-making. If a leader is serious about his or her company's values, that leader has to reinforce the seriousness of those values by demonstrating how they have a practical day-to-day application.

Above all, the leader must demonstrate these values in his or her own dealings. By all accounts, Steve Jobs was not an easy person to know or get along with; but he certainly embodied all of Apple's values, and he built a company consistent with those values.

HLAs

You have a vision, you have set the goals needed to make that vision a reality, and you have a set of values you believe are the right ones for your company. You also have a plan to communicate your vision and values and show your team members how to translate these values into everyday work. Now it is time to take the final step.

It starts with conveying the concept of leverage. Yes, everyone knows what leverage is in the physical sense; but it is important to communicate how leverage works in terms of tasks. Your people need to think in terms of leverage applied to their to-do lists and the pursuit of their job-related goals. They need to understand how the company vision is used as the measuring stick and how values are used in selecting HLAs.

The goal for every member of your company from top to bottom is to "think" in terms of prioritization by *High Leverage Activities* without even realizing they are doing so. In other words, we want every member of your organization or team to work in HLA-thinking as their default mode. We want them to speak the "language" of an HLA culture. In an HLA culture no one should consciously have to think about HLAs. It should just be second nature.

If you live inside a culture, your behavioral norms aren't something you think about or are even aware of. It is just the way things are. You are like the fish in water. The fish isn't aware of the water. It is just the way things are. That's how a High Leverage culture should be. Working in HLAs should be second nature.

> IF YOU LIVE INSIDE A CULTURE, YOUR BEHAVIORAL NORMS AREN'T SOMETHING YOU THINK ABOUT OR ARE EVEN AWARE OF. IT IS JUST THE WAY THINGS ARE. YOU ARE LIKE THE FISH IN WATER. THE FISH ISN'T AWARE OF THE WATER. IT IS JUST THE WAY THINGS ARE. THAT'S HOW A HIGH LEVERAGE CULTURE SHOULD BE. WORKING IN HLAS SHOULD BE SECOND NATURE.

We will spend the next two chapters looking at exactly how a leader should make the HLA concept a part of his or her everyday approach. Then we will look at how each and every individual should use the HLA concept on the job every day. Once the HLA concept has permeated every level of your organization, you will have achieved the HLA culture. And you will see your results meter moving ever faster.

VIPs

1. Corporate culture is real and critical to achieving vision. Being intentional about the culture you create will affect your ability to achieve and exceed your goals.
2. An organizational culture should be built on a shared and accepted vision, mutual and widely accepted values, behavioral norms, and accepted levels of accomplishment.
3. Vision Boards are the starting place to build a culture. These are graphic representations of your vision and your values. They provide a constant reminder to all of your stakeholders as to what you're going to achieve and how you're going to achieve it.
4. Once HLAs become a part of the culture, working in HLAs should just be second nature.

CHAPTER 8
A LEADER'S GUIDE TO HLAs

*"The best way to achieve extraordinary results is
to become intentional about being strategic."*
-Tony Jeary

As a leader of a division, department, and any kind of team, you pretty much know and accept the company vision. The company values are values you believe will enhance your team's performance, will give them pride in belonging to the organization, and provide day-to-day guidance in decision making. You know the company's goals, and you have determined the goals both you and your team need to achieve with at least an approximate timeframe for their achievement. Now you need to know the specific results you will need to accomplish to meet your goals.

Let's start this process with the results you are getting today. Make a list of your key metrics (what you can measure) and look at the results they represent. Then make a side-by-side list of the results needed to meet your new goals. What's the delta, or gap? This shouldn't need to involve a lot of sophisticated software. This is something you need to be able to do with a legal pad and a pen, or even just on your phone. Keep it quick and simple (under ten items).

(Note: In some cases, there will be no comparisons to make. You may have great sales results for a product that is going to be discontinued, so there is no desired future result. Or you may have no history for a new product soon to be introduced. In the latter case, your base is obviously zero. This is important because it could mean a total reallocation of resources.)

Now ask yourself: "What do I need to do to close the performance gap?" If it is a new endeavor, the gap is what is between zero and your needed future results. That is automatically a huge gap.

If you lead a sales team, you will have to look carefully at your current results. Just because you have regularly hit your sales goals in the past doesn't mean you are ready to produce the results needed to achieve the company vision. In the short run, the vision might require discontinuing some lines of business to focus on others with higher margins or lower production costs.

If you are a service leader, your goals may include shorter response times, lower costs, and a dramatic lowering of return visits. This may involve creating new training, installing new mobile software systems, and creating collaboration tools. It also may involve lots of new recruiting and possibly reducing the head count in other areas—something that is often unpleasant. **(Note: Investing time in C and D minus-level players is often an LLA, a Low Level Activity).**

If you are in marketing, it may mean repositioning the brand. All of this represents change that will require new ways of thinking different types of results than you may be used to. Whatever your goals, you need to understand how your results have to change. And your team has to understand that, too.

The next step is to look closely at the gaps. Then list the steps you believe must be taken to achieve each desired result. You now have a model for closing the gaps. You know what needs to be done. And you have an idea of when it needs to be done.

It is a fact of life that every leader and manager has certain limited resources for any given point in time. There is only so much money and so much time. This makes discretionary time and money a treasure to be carefully used to achieve the tasks required, which will move the needle toward the goals that will ultimately build the vision.

Today even small organizations use software to track progress, monitor expenditures, and measure results. But it all really comes down to the old-fashioned "to-do" list. What do you need to accomplish today, and what tasks do you need to complete to get the job done? From the leaders' perspective, it is about determining which tasks need to be accomplished first and then allocating the resources of time, money, and effort to get the job done.

Not everything can be done at once, so you must set priorities. Which tasks need to be accomplished first? Sometimes the answer is obvious. Sometimes one task cannot be accomplished until another is finished, so the order is clear. But leaders with a goal to achieve usually face the unenviable challenge of trying to determine the priority of a to-do list. Then they have to train their subordinates or direct reports how to organize their own to-do list in some degree of harmony.

> IN AN HLA COMPANY THERE IS A CLEAR VISION TO GUIDE DECISION-MAKING. GOALS AT ALL LEVELS ARE SET ACCORDING TO WHAT IS NEEDED TO ACHIEVE THE AGREED-UPON VISION.

All too often this is done on an ad-hoc basis. The leader looks to his or her perceived own best interest. Corporate politics is a key factor. Personal likes and dislikes play a part. *Blind Spots* in our thinking really come into play, too. But in the HLA company there is a clear vision to guide decision-making. Goals at all levels are set according to what is needed to achieve the agreed-upon vision.

Values are clear, and they set the parameters of action. You won't ever totally purge politics or personalities from your operations, but you can achieve standards for judgment that reduce these factors to a minimum.

Now the trick is to allocate the resources of time, money, and effort to those tasks that will drive the results you need in the shortest time possible. As you start this exercise, keep in mind that your time is one of the most valuable assets you have. Time is limited. You can't do the entire job yourself; but in a time of transition you will have to play an active management role in all key projects. Spread yourself too thin and you will likely fall short. Work a hundred hours a week, and your life is likely to fall apart.

Your first step is making a simple task list. What are the tasks that need to get done to achieve your goals in the required time frame? Make the list on paper, or simply type it into an email on your phone to yourself, but don't worry about the order just yet.

Then under each task create a "to-do" list of the things that have to be accomplished by someone to achieve those tasks. Again, just make a list; it doesn't need to be in any particular order. After you have completed the to-do list, create a start date and a completion date for each task. Now assign team members to each task and break up the to-do list by individual. Then estimate the amount of time each will require to finish their job. There will be instances where one team member can't finish a job until receiving input from another team member or someone outside the team. Calculate likely lost time from these wait times. Again, don't forget to estimate your own time commitment to each task. Finally, assign a cost estimate to each task.

You should now have a decent overview of what your team has to do and the rough amount of resources required. Make this exercise fit your outcome. So far your calculations are based on estimated metrics. They are simple estimates to be sure, with some insights and experience; they are likely not too far off. Review your work. Does something not feel right? Question everything. Are you being overly optimistic about time requirements? Are you fudging estimates because you don't think you have what is really required? Is there a reliance on an outside contractor or vendor, or even another internal department that you know in your gut won't perform as needed? This is a time for brutal honesty. Once you have made this gut check, adjust numbers as you think necessary.

The next step is a once-over for the people component. Look carefully at your personnel assignments. We all know there are lots of people who are very competent at their jobs who nevertheless need constant guidance. There are self-starters and people who need a nudge. There are good people who nevertheless have focus issues. There are cheerleaders. Consider carefully the mix of personalities. Properly balancing talents and personalities can make a difference in the speed of the team's result. It can also make a huge difference in the allocation of your personal time. You may want to make some adjustments.

Another key component as a leader is to be realistic about what can be achieved. Just saying you want or need something doesn't make it possible. Set up your team to win, and put the resources in place to help make it happen. Yes, you need to provide challenging goals and stretch goals and not accept pedestrian achievement. After all, you have a vision to make a reality. Don't set yourself up for failure by kidding yourself, your boss, or your team about what is really possible with the resources available. You can ask your people to give you eighty hours a week, but that won't give you twice the results of forty hours a week. In fact, it may give you less. Buying a software system you know to be inadequate because you can afford it won't get you where you need to go. You have to be realistic.

Once you have made a truly realistic assessment of the resources required, you need to look at the outputs required and expected and the timelines you have to work with. Where are you getting the greatest movement for the investment?

Pretty straight forward isn't it? Maybe it's not. Here is one thing you may not have considered at all. Which tasks are most visible to important stakeholders? Has your team fully bought in to the company vision? Do they believe it is attainable? Chances are there is some skepticism. So it is important to quickly gain the confidence of your team in the company's vision. Do your investors have confidence in the vision and the ability of the company to execute? Maybe your

> VISIBLY WALK YOUR WALK. THE RESULTS SPEAK FOR THEMSELVES. DONE RIGHT, THE MOST IMPORTANT COMMUNICATION VEHICLE A COMPANY HAS WILL BE WORKING OVERTIME FOR YOU: THE MOUTH BUZZ NEAR THE WATER COOLER.

customers are fearful that change will not be good for them. The quickest way to dispel doubts is to follow Nike's slogan—just do it. Start executing your role as an amazing leader of the goals and vision and manage the details of the teams under you with HLAs and MOLO.

Visibly walk the walk. The results speak for themselves. Done right, the most important communication vehicle a company has will be working overtime for you: the mouth buzz near the water cooler.

People know when they score, and they will be the first to talk about it. Keep in mind that the real opinion leaders among your people are probably unknown to you. Their ability to sway internal, or even external, opinion has nothing to do with their title or the size of their paycheck. They are simply people who other people listen to and heed. When the buzz is positive, and even at the "Wow" level, you'll find that your entire organization will visibly notice a change in attitude.

This isn't to say visibility is a hard and fast rule of HLAs. It is to say you should consider the potential leverage of starting the journey to your vision with wins that are highly visible to create credibility across your stakeholder community. It is also nice to know the rumor mill is working for you, not against you.

Beyond visibility let's consider what HLAs might be. Delta Dental is the largest dental benefits company in the United States, providing dental coverage to more than 60 million people with $18 billion in annual premium revenue. Delta's executive, Rob Budd, explains how his company realized that sales "presentations" were an HLA. They didn't need to spend a lot of time and money to overhaul their presentations, but the results were dramatic. "We make very strategic presentations that focus on our customer's needs and that help us connect in a very powerful way," explains Budd. "Anyone can sell on price and product. But we now use a presentation approach focused on value and the real needs of our prospects."

What Robb and Delta Dental did was "find the need behind the need." Yes, their prospects needed dental health insurance, but why did they need this coverage? "Previously we responded to questions," explains Budd, "but now we invest serious time in investigating the real needs on the front end and dig deep." What the company needed was better and faster sales results for what were highly complex high-dollar sales with lots of decision makers involved. By focusing resources earlier on in the sales cycle, Delta was able to create more sales faster.

In evaluating their activities to select their HLAs, the executives at Delta Dental asked the simple question: What do we need more of and what do we need less of (MOLO)? What they needed was more sales and a shorter sales cycle. They also needed a way to differentiate themselves instead of solely selling based on price or product features, which are fairly standardized in their industry. What they needed less of was slow progress and those moving forward at a snail's pace.

At the HP University Joanne Moretti wanted to drive home how the *High Leverage Activity* could be used at the team level to gain results. "HP is a mammoth organization which means success rests on managers taking the initiative to hit their goals," she explains. "Our goal was to provide an organizing principle that allowed managers to see their job as sustainable results. That means better results with fewer resources. The HLA concept provided that organizing principle for mid-level action."

If you are a sales leader, think about your sales process. What are your bottlenecks? Where do you get hung up? Do you often find your efforts grinding to a halt due to your client's corporate politics? Are there decision makers at the table you didn't expect? What are you really selling?

The MOLO approach to HLAs will guide you to the leverage points in your cycle. Solving a bottleneck may cost you considerable resources for minimal gain. Changing a commodity approach to a value approach may produce significant results for virtually no resource cost at all.

As you look across the few pages of notes you have created to identify your HLAs, your instincts will kick in. Don't shrug them off. It isn't always about the algorithms. It is about you using your knowledge, experience, and judgment to put numbers on those to-do lists and bring maximum leverage of resources to bear at the point where they will advance the needle fastest.

VIPs

1. Make certain you are clear on your organization's vision and overall goals. Make certain that your team's vision and goals are in alignment and that you fully grasp what you and your team need to do and by when to carry your part of the load.

2. Make a list of your key metrics (what you can measure) and look at the results they represent. Then make a side-by-side list of the results needed to meet your new goals. What's the gap? Then ask yourself what it is you need to close that gap.

3. Look for the why behind the what. The problem isn't that sales are lagging; that's a symptom. You have to look for the reason sales are down. That's the illness.

4. Make a list of the tasks you need to accomplish to close gaps and achieve the goals that will achieve the vision. Then prioritize them based on what will drive the results you need the fastest. This exercise helps you identify activities driven by politics, or that are simply one-off efforts. Everything must be judged by the North Star of the common vision.

5. Assign each task an estimated amount of time and money needed to complete it. You will quickly see the tradeoffs. The activity that moves your needle the farthest may suck more resources than it's worth. The objective is to achieve the most impactful use of resources, or, put another way, the maximum leverage.

6. Always consider what you will need from others and their ability to provide it on your needed timetable. Conversely, consider what others need from you. If their needs represent importance for the organization, meeting their needs becomes an HLA.

7. Consider visibility to stakeholders. Quick wins can create a high level of confidence with your team, with other teams, and with outside stakeholders that are critical to achieving the vision. Quick wins can attract greater resources from headquarters, too, as their confidence in your leadership grows.

8. Keep the concept of MOLO in mind. "What do I need more of and what can I use less of?" There is no better way to assess your HLAs as a leader than to apply the MOLO concept.

CHAPTER 9
MEASURE EVERYTHING

"What gets measured gets managed."
-PETER DRUCKER, RECIPIENT OF THE
PRESIDENTIAL MEDAL OF FREEDOM

"Accountability is the magic of exceptional leadership."
-TONY JEARY

The great Management thinker Peter Drucker coined the phrase "You cannot manage what you cannot measure." This is true in both business and life. Every morning a personal trainer comes to my home gym and we work on strength training, cardiovascular, flexibility, and other aspects of conditioning. In some cases it is about maintenance; there is a limit to how much I will ever be able to lift or lose (weight/inches). In some cases I've likely hit that limit, but in other areas I have plenty of room left for improvement. I didn't reach my limits overnight. It took months, and in some cases years, of incremental improvement with a ton of focus and sweat to get where I wanted to go.

What was perhaps the most important thing on this fitness journey was to know where I was and where I wanted to go so I could see week-to-week that I was making progress. In fitness you can often hit plateaus. No matter how hard you work you just don't make progress. That doesn't mean you have hit your limits (although it might); it means you need to give your body time to adjust and prepare for the next leap forward. None of this is possible if you don't have goals and don't measure your progress session by session.

The same is true in business. A startup rarely goes from zero to $100 million in a year. (It does happen; Compaq Computer did.) And the bigger you grow your percentage gains get smaller. When a company does achieve a hyper-high growth rate, they often find themselves overwhelmed by unanticipated consequences. They lack the capacity or skilled workers, their capital structures don't fit the reality, their computer systems are overwhelmed, and their cultural development develops disease. Growth for its own sake becomes the goal, and the company fails to develop a supportive infrastructure and culture.

Whether your vision encompasses growth or profitability or both, or other factors, you have to take time to ensure that your vision is sustainable. That means realistically measuring the resources required to get where you want to go and faithfully measuring your progress toward those goals. It means time and money. You have to understand the relative value of what you're investing. That requires measurement. It makes no sense to commit to a course of action that will devour resources to the point that other critical tasks fail to get done.

As we know, this is what *High Leverage Activities* are all about: How much relative progress for how much investment of resources.

To know how much investment of resources you need, you have to know where you are starting, often in terms of numbers. You have to know where you want to go, again often in terms of numbers. You have to calculate the gap. As I have said, goals (objectives) are the building blocks of your vision. The goals (objectives) must be measureable in numbers. It could be cost savings or most likely growth of your organization in sales, income, and profits. This might mean higher levels of quality. How do you measure quality? There has to be a metric that defines a start and a finish, as well as progress.

It is the job of a strong leader to assure realism in numbers. Human nature is to fudge bad news and exaggerate good news. Is the starting point really as good as advertised? A manager may look good on the front end by asserting a robust starting position, but it will only make it harder to reach the goals if that starting point was false bravado. The willingness of a division or department head to set high goals may make them look good out of the gate, but they won't look so good when they fail to deliver because they never really stood a chance.

It is the job of a good leader to build a culture that values accuracy and realism. We have all heard the old joke about the man interviewing accountants who asks them the single question: "What is the sum of two plus two? One applicant after another answers "four" and is instantly dismissed. Finally, one applicant answers, "What do you want it to be?" and gets the job. That happens all too often in organizational life. We want a number to be 10, so we assign the person who says they can hit 10, whether that is realistic or not. Be real.

It is also critical to measure the right things. Increasing presentations or sales calls doesn't matter if the conversion/closing ratio goes down and overall revenue falls. Well-estimated resource consumption doesn't matter if resources aren't providing the needed results.

You have to get to the why behind the what. That means carefully considering the metrics you are going to use to measure progress. Ask yourself: Is this too much data, or is this real actionable information? The information leaders need answers to strategic questions.

When you identify what you believe to be a *High Leverage Activity*, you evaluate the output relative to the inputs. Did it work out as you thought it would? Or were more resources consumed than you estimated? Did you move the needle as far as you expected? Was the task completed on time? If you were wrong, why were you wrong and where were you wrong? There is no point in kidding yourself. Be honest with yourself. Leaders take responsibility for their actions and decisions; and when the results fail to measure up, they find out why without bias so they can make needed corrections.

Accuracy in Measurement (AIM) is a part of an HLA culture. *High Leverage Activities* as an organizing principle won't work well unless you can effectively measure progress in closing gaps between where you are and where you need to go and progress toward your goals and objectives. This is as true for the bottom of an organization as it is for the top. Mid-level managers can't make HLAs work without the right metrics, because they won't be able to evaluate their progress. Individuals won't be able to use HLAs if they don't know how many hours they spend on a project. No leaders will do their best unless they measure.

It's that simple!

Leaders need clarity of more than their vision. They need clarity of reality and the will and confidence to accept reality. You may nudge the golf ball in the hole when no one is looking and claim your first par four on Hole 12; but the truth is, you made it in five. Maybe it doesn't cause grief on the golf course, but it sure will in an organization.

If managers, team members, and associates are afraid to tell the truth, the leaders won't get the truth. But if all stakeholders understand that leadership will accept nothing but accuracy and that candor is to be rewarded, they will respond at all levels. It is up to leaders throughout the organization to instill the value of truth and accuracy as a key cultural value.

Another critical benefit to accurate measurements arises when measurements are shared. One of the most frequent complaints I hear from management teams is about "silos." Companies, especially larger companies, are divided into divisions and departments that often keep information to themselves. In part this is because information is power. In part this is because it is easier to fudge the numbers. In large part it is just human nature to keep cards close to the vest. But it can also be destructive. Secretiveness not only pits one part of an organization against another part, it frequently means a lack of information to effectively identify and implement HLAs.

Frequently information needed for the service division to efficiently meet its goals requires knowledge of sales that sales wants to keep to itself. Product development teams want to avoid having marketing run too far out in front of them. Yet it is almost impossible to utilize HLAs as an organizing principle without the right information and the right measurements. Leadership has to work to break down these walls by using the HLA concept to require the sharing of critical information. As team members at all levels begin to think in terms of HLAs and MOLO and AIM, they will become more open to sharing of information, because they will see that dramatic progress benefiting all will result.

Another essential use for metrics or the scorecard approach is the ability to compare like teams. Let's say we have three sales teams all with the same goals. If one sales team meets its objectives and another blows them away and the third lags far behind, it is important to know why they performed as they did. Common measurements are the only way. The reason may be as simple as the A Team being composed of veterans and the C Team of newbies. Or maybe it is the potential of the territories assigned. Or it may be a matter of leadership. Team A may have grasped and fully implemented the HLA concept while the C Team didn't. That would be a good point of comparison to get lagging teams across the board to buy in. But there may be other reasons that will show up in the measurements /scorecards. If you can pinpoint the "why" behind the "what," you can fix the problem.

One trait the best leaders I have worked with possess is an innate understanding that you can only go as far as you can see, but when you get there you will be able to see farther. In other words, be careful about setting goals and objectives you don't know if you can meet. Goal setting is about increments. Vision is way out there and includes often who you want to become one day, way out there. My personal goal may have been to have a 31-inch waist one day, but it sure wasn't my goal to do so after three workouts. There were a lot of "one-pound-more," "one more inch" week-to-week goals in between the gap where I started and 31 inches around the middle. Your stakeholders may not be able to see how you are going to make the leap from the present to your vision, but they can see how you can get from the starting gate to the first turn. Set the first turn as your goal and use your measurements to take you there. When you get there, take a look at the straightaway. Accurate measurements will help you adjust your goals and objectives and better identify your HLAs going into that straightaway.

Let's switch now from organizational measurement to individual measurement. Let's start at the beginning by finding out the individual's starting point. The way to do this is with assessments. Having the right leadership and the right team members is a HUGE requirement for getting results. When I work with top performers to help them go from good to great and from great to mastery, I start with an assessment centered on leadership best practices. In fact, I published a mini book on it. It's called *The Leadership 25*. It's made up of 25 absolute characteristics of a powerful leader, taken from all the leaders I've coached over the years, including the presidents of Ford, Walmart, New York Life, Firestone, Samsung, and more. I start by having the individual rate themselves from 1 to 4 in these 25 areas. It's quick and it's powerful for finding the gaps quickly on where I can best guide, support, and advise. (For a free copy, email my organization, Tony Jeary International, at info@tonyjeary.com, and we'll get a copy to you.)

The right assessments can measure leadership ability and future potential, time management, meeting effectiveness, problem solving abilities or almost any other objective you might have. Assessments are a powerful tool and should be used to guide your recruiting, allocate resources, and even in making assignments. Obviously, they can also be used to provide vital information about strengths and weaknesses that individuals can use to shore up their weaknesses.

Let me also introduce you to another special tool. I partnered with HRDQ and developed an assessment called Strategic Acceleration Quotient (SAQ). The purpose of this assessment, being more robust (about 20 to 30 minutes of time investment), was to determine an individual's abilities and skills to drive results fast, based on the strategic acceleration methodology of clarity, focus, and execution. Basically, how likely are they to quickly achieve clarity of vision and purpose? How capable are they of saying "no" to distractions and focusing on the task at hand? How capable are they of executing? (This is, of course, a way of asking how capable they are of identifying an HLA.) This assessment, too, is a measurement tool that organizations and individuals can use to build their HLA culture. (Take the assessment at www.saqassessment.com)

Individuals also need to be able to measure their progress from where they are to where they need to go to achieve their vision for themselves. This can mean acquiring or improving the skills needed to thrive in an HLA culture. It can also mean measuring the extent to which they have learned to say "no" to distractions. Besides focus up front, another nice thing about assessments is that they can be used to measure progress. As individuals work in an HLA culture and speak the language of MOLO and AIM, their skills will improve. It is important that individuals be able to measure their progress, and it is important for their leaders to know progress is being made.

I've published over 40 books in the past two decades, and "measurement" is a real trend in my content. A time management book I wrote 17 years ago titled *How to Get 100 Extra Minutes a Day* is still an exceptional book that is based around measuring where you really are day-in and day-out. This book has empowered thousands of people to literally gain 100 extra minutes each day to use as they needed. Measurement was the key, because you cannot manage what you cannot measure in any endeavor.

Bottom line: It's not enough to put some new things into action, lay out the things you say you will do, and just go about doing them. It is critical to measure the individual and collective effectiveness so you can continue to make adjustments, do more of what is working, and do less of what is not working. Working in HLAs is a journey, not a destination. There is always a next level; and as the world changes, the way we all do business must change. If not, our competitors will take over our competitive advantages if they are willing to change.

Working in HLAs is a mindset. It creates clarity of what is important. It supports a culture focused on productivity based on the right things, and it is about executing for exponential results *FASTER*.

VIPs

1. "You cannot manage what you cannot measure," said the father of management science, Peter Drucker. In an HLA culture, measurement is the essential—almost sacred—ingredient.
2. You need to know where you are, where you need to go, and what the gap is you have to close, *in terms of numbers.*
3. Accuracy in Measurements (AIM) is as integral to using HLAs as MOLO or TOM. Reality is what it is, and you have to know. No fudging, and no fooling yourself. Leadership demands reality, and that is the only way it can get a clear picture.
4. You have to measure the right things. That requires knowing the why behind the what.
5. A common metrics system provides the basis for common analysis. It lets you see why one team is running far ahead and an identical team is lagging behind.
6. Always measure the increments. You want to know if you are making progress toward the finish line, not just when you cross the line.
7. Assessments are an excellent way to measure starting points and progress for almost any category. Excellent assessment products exist for almost anything you want to measure about your organization or your people.
8. Measuring allows you to make the necessary adjustments as needed to continue to succeed.

TAKEAWAYS - PART FIVE

PART SIX
YOUR PERSONAL SUCCESS

*"The quality of a person's life is in direct proportion
to their commitment to excellence."*
-VINCE LOMBARDI

O ur final section is all about you. How do you carry the many concepts we have discussed in this book into your everyday life? I mean by this your personal life and your professional life.

Everyone talks a lot about work and life balance, and it is an essential concept to health and happiness as well as to your personal goals. The fact is that we only have so much time, whether we invest it on the pursuit of financial goals, our kids, our spiritual lives, or our marriages. How do we allocate our time in a manner that allows us to be successful in every area of our lives?

I submit that the *High Leverage Activity* concept is the way forward to achieve success across the board. Life requires constant adjustment. Sometimes work simply demands a greater percentage of our available time if we are to meet our goals. At other times work must simply give way to the needs of family or friends for our own mental or spiritual well-being.

The good news is, if your vision of what you want in life is clear, you have a guide to your needs. A clear vision will help create clear goals. And clear goals will guide you in allocating your time, your emotional energy, and other resources to reaching those goals. Yes, those goals will change throughout your life. Review your HLAs often. Sometimes just small adjustments are needed, and other times you need to completely change the items on your list. That requires a rebalancing of priorities and time. **The HLA concept will help you through those rebalancing activities and continue to drive you toward success.**

CHAPTER 10
MODEL IT AS A LEADER

"The enemy of mastery is often greatness."
-TONY JEARY

HLAs aren't just for corporate planning, organizations, or team management. The concept is every bit as valid (perhaps even more) for individual leaders in planning and executing their specific role and their overall lives. It doesn't matter if you are the CEO or receptionist or front line manager. The HLA concept moves all needles, and all needles need to move.

We have looked at creating an overall HLA culture and at how leaders can use the HLA methodology to move their organization's needles to the desired position. Now we want to look at how one person can use the HLA method-

> IT DOESN'T MATTER IF YOU ARE THE CEO OR RECEPTIONIST OR FRONT LINE MANAGER. THE HLA CONCEPT MOVES ALL NEEDLES, AND ALL NEEDLES NEED TO MOVE.

ology to become more productive as a leader.

What all of us have in common is an absolute limit on time. You have to sleep sometime (this should be 56 hours a week). You have to have a shower, brush your teeth, comb your hair, get dressed; so plug in 12 hours a week for maintenance to round out the numbers. So 168 hours in a week, minus 56 for sleep, minus 12 for maintenance, leaves you with 100 hours; 50 for professional and 50 or so for personal.

Now for you as an individual, the goal is greater utilization of your time to produce the right results faster. As an individual, you need to start the same as an entire organization: with clarity of vision. What do you need/want to accomplish?

An individual's HLA program should start with MOLO. What do you need more of and what can you do with less of? I want to re-emphasize how important the language of MOLO is. It is a Tony Jeary principle that works like magic. MOLO clarifies an often muddled world. Maybe you need more time to think. Maybe you need more time to work on a sales presentation. Maybe it's coaching others you need time for. Maybe as CEO you need more time to consider acquisition opportunities to attain your vision. You only have so much time, so what can you use less of to gain the time required?

In terms of organizing your personal work agenda, the objective is to keep in mind what you want to accomplish individually. What do you want professionally, as an individual (for your brand/reputation to grow)? What do you want for your skill sets? How could you get more connections or better leverage the ones you have? How would you like your income to grow?

Ask yourself: Among the many demands on my time, which ones will produce the results needed to achieve the goals that will make my goals/vision a reality? Write them down.

Then begin to consider how much of your time each week you should invest in that item. I suggest you pick 4 to 8 professional HLAs that apply to your current role and professional goals. Here are mine:

Professional HLAs

1. Attract strong, qualified clients.
2. Deliver extraordinary value to our clients.
3. Clarify our direction as the founder of our firm.
4. Gain wisdom (study); especially since I'm in the wisdom business, I'd better be growing my own arsenal from which to pull.
5. Nourish my connections.

So when something comes into my life that requires even minutes, I ask myself, "Is it something that trumps my HLAs or is an "aha" that I need to stop and pay attention to immediately?" If not, then I most likely will pass. Now, there are many exceptions. And it is also unrealistic to think you can work 100% within your HLAs. The goal is to spend the bulk of your time in HLAs and organize your time in such a way that you can efficiently handle those necessary items that are LLAs without giving them an inappropriate amount of time and attention. The key point, again, is that an HLA focus helps filter tasks or commitments out.

Let me provide an example I often share from the stage:

Mike calls me and says, "Tony, how about lunch?" I ask myself if this is an HLA. I know this will require a minimum of two hours of my time. Then I decide, based on HLA thinking, to dig deeper. "Mike, what's on your mind?" He says, "I want to meet Jill, and you know her well." I tell him that, instead of lunch I will email and connect the two of them together. She's a friend and we're connected, so I can easily make that happen. Mike is happy! I invested 7 minutes instead of 120. Now that's HLA thinking that you and everyone else can relate to. If you're clear on your HLAs, both personally and professionally, you can better manage those 100 hours we all have.

Now back to your list of HLAs. Go ahead and write it now. List 4 to 8 activities

> WITHOUT CLARITY YOU MISS THE PULLING POWER NEEDED TO INVEST YOUR TIME IN HLAs.

that are professional and 4 to 8 activities that are personal. Then out to the side put the approximate amount of hours per week you think you need to spend on each item. The total should be about 35 hours, or 70 percent of the 50 hours allocated to that side of your life. This will allow margin for necessary activities outside your HLAs and things you cannot foresee that will invariably come up to address. (I know there's overlap, but you get the exercise.) It's simple, yet most aren't that clear on the concept. Without clarity you miss the pulling power needed to invest your time in HLAs. Trust me; this works. If I were your personal coach, I would have you type both HLA lists in your phone.

How much time do you have? If your *Highest Leverage Activity* will require greater time than you can currently give, you need to identify the *Low Leverage Activities* that are sucking time and cut them, or at least cut back. Then perhaps ask, what can you offload to your team members? What can you outsource? Yes, outsourcing to consultants, assistants, interns, lawyers, bookkeepers, etc. can be expensive; but if your time is absolutely required to tackle your *Highest Leverage Activity,* it can be money well invested. It doesn't even have to be everything, but everything you get off your plate frees up your time for other high leverage things.

After hearing me speak about this for years, my business manager put this concept to the test in her personal life. She now has other people do many things that are necessary but not necessary for her. By having other people run errands, connect with outside vendors for home maintenance needs, shop for groceries, take their car to the shop, etc., she has determined the value back to her has freed her up in two ways—to better focus on her HLAs at work and to capture back some free time that was sorely missing in her home/work balance. This may be an area where you can change your thinking and create some incremental success.

You do have to look at the big picture, which means you have to be keenly aware of what others need from you to do their jobs. How highly leveraged is their task in regard to the vision? If it is more critical to achieving the overall vision, your highest leverage activity may well be finishing a project that will let others get on with their job. Of course, your opinion of the importance of what they are doing and their opinion may differ. That is where negotiation and communication skills come in.

The good news is that when you and your colleagues are speaking the language of HLAs, and are both clear on the guiding vision and the MOLO concept, you have a common ground to communicate and settle those issues. Otherwise, it is just a test of wills and a battle to prove who has the clout. No one wins those tugs of war. But when you are guided by common values and have a common HLA approach, there is a common denominator for working things out.

Even budgeting issues can be worked through. Maybe another department has excess budget. Good for them. To accomplish your goals, you may absolutely need more dollars. Your colleague has them. Normal corporate procedure may be to spend every dime, even if it is wasted.

But in an HLA culture, it is far easier to work these things out for the common good.

Calculating resources required versus output isn't the exact science it may seem. There is art involved here, too. But starting with clarity of mission will provide guidance. Using the MOLO concept to get a high-level feel will move you well down the road. Judging the estimated inputs and outputs injects an element of metrics, even if approximate. When this exercise is complete, you will have a pretty good sense of what your to-do list should look like.

Now let's face it, your priority list will change as new facts arise and circumstances change. If you can get through a single day with an unaltered list, you are an unusual person. My own list usually changes several times in a day. Because I think in terms of HLAs and because MOLO has become an almost subconscious reaction, I can usually make adjustments on the fly pretty easily.

The truth is, flexibility isn't something that comes easy to most of us. We have our plans made and are reluctant to change them. Change disrupts our lives and the lives of people working for us or our families.

Usually we spend a lot of time trying to maintain the original plan of action. What causes pain is an ad-hoc approach. Using the HLA method allows us to quickly determine if a reordering of our list is really necessary or not. If it is, the reordering is a lot easier, because we know it has to be done and we know how to do the reordering. The common language of the HLA also allows us to communicate quickly and succinctly the "why" to others who have to change their own priorities.

Again, let me repeat that MOLO and HLAs also apply to our personal lives. Using HLAs as an organizing principle for our personal to-do lists and MOLO as a thought process can help us achieve more of what we want in our personal lives, lower overall stress, and free up time for a more productive professional life.

It starts, as I keep saying here, with being really clear about what you want from life. If you are married, I hope that a happy, fulfilling partnership with your spouse is something you want more of. If you have children, I hope that helping them grow up into happy, well-balanced adults with good judgment and values is a clear goal. There is nothing wrong with having financial goals, either. There is nothing wrong with wanting a nice home, or a pool, or being able to take rewarding vacations. Or maybe what you want is more time to engage in fly-fishing or fun travel. What you want isn't so much the point as your being honest with yourself and your loved ones about what it is you really want. I can assure you, if you don't know you won't achieve it.

Without question our goals change as we age and experience more of life. A single person in their twenties may be very clear that they want to get married and start a family. Twenty years later, married and with kids, the goals are likely to turn toward financial and lifestyle goals. At some point, financial security for mature years becomes a goal. At every point in your life you have to be thinking about your goals.

My friend Bob Buford wrote a very impactful book called *Half Time* in which he talked about what successful people should do with their lives once they had achieved success. Buford's book was the outgrowth of a personal tragedy, the loss of his college-age son who had drowned while swimming the Rio Grande River to experience what Mexican immigrants experienced. The event caused Buford to reassess his life goals. He had made money, but had decades left to use his many talents and his experience to achieve new goals. Many of us hit this point in life where it seems time to make a new to-do list that has little in common with our old lists.

What better way to arrive at a new life vision than applying the MOLO concept. If you want to spend more time with your family, then you need to figure out what you want less of to make that time. Maybe you have a daughter who plays tennis. You aren't half bad at the game yourself. Would you like to find the time to play more tennis with your daughter? Maybe you will decide that you can spend less time watching TV or going out to dinner. Maybe you have a longing to develop a neglected spiritual life. You realize you haven't been to church in years because you have been too busy building a successful career. But times have changed, and you feel something is missing. If you have a clear vision of your life with greater spiritual meaning, then you need to decide what you want less of to make the time.

> THE IDEA OF A LIFE AND WORK BALANCE ISN'T JUST A CATCH PHRASE. IT IS THE WAY TO SUCCESS AND HAPPINESS.

Very few of us can partition our lives to the point we can leave professional problems at the office, even the home office, or home problems at home. One impacts the other. The idea of a life and work balance isn't just a catch phrase. It is the way to success with happiness.

VIPs

1. HLAs and the concept of MOLO aren't just for organizations or executives, or even leaders. The concept works for everyone at every level—day in and day out, at work and in our personal lives.

2. All of us have about 50 hours each week for our professional activities and another 50 hours each week for our personal lives. The objective is to utilize that limited time for activities that will advance you toward your goals and avoid distractions or waste.

3. Ask yourself, "Among the many demands on my time, which ones will produce the most results needed to achieve the goals that will make my goals/vision a reality?" Write them down. Then consider how much of your time each week you should invest in each item.

4. Find ways to do tasks with less time. Instead of a lunch meeting, will a phone call or even an email do instead?

5. Off-load or outsource what makes sense. Is the cost of outsourcing more or less than the cost of your time? Don't be afraid to delegate.

6. Life is about tradeoffs. When you determine that you need more of something (your limited time or other resources) than you currently have, determine what you can do with less of and make the shift.

7. Flexibility isn't something that comes naturally. When we have a plan, we want to stick to it. But circumstances change—often by the hour. This requires a constant reappraisal of what really are our HLAs versus what aren't, and an adjustment of our master to-do list.

8. As we age and our circumstances change, our goals change (or should); and that requires a rethinking of our vision and goals. With the clarity of a new vision and goals, we have to adjust our HLAs to meet new challenges and opportunities.

CONCLUSION

Leadership is a results contest … meaning that winning leaders must drive superior results faster and faster. One of the things I have learned from 25 years of coaching the best executives and high achievers in the world is that they grasp and use the concept of leverage. They leverage resources, assets, experiences, opportunities, location, people, processes, and time. The main takeaway from this book is that leverage is the driver of results. To win, you have to get better and better at using leverage. To take it one step farther, the most successful and the most respected leaders are also the ones who are open-minded to changing their thinking. They are the ones who get exponential results time and time again.

> **THE ANSWER TO LEVERAGING TIME IS A LASER FOCUS ON HLAS.**

It is key to remember that time is the key differentiator in both your personal life and in business. How you leverage time will determine your results, your success, and whether or not you are winning the leadership contest.

The answer to leveraging time is a laser focus on HLAs.

In today's fast-paced world, top performers lead with clarity and reprioritize often. Top leaders have clarity of the 6 or 8 or 10 things that will most move their results needle. They get laser focused on organizational HLAs. They get their people laser focused. They think about HLAs every day, and even every hour, and make sure everyone is zeroed in on doing what matters most as a team: the organization's HLAs.

The same goes for individuals. Every person on your team can waste time and effort or be laser focused on tasks that move the needle. All individuals on your team should know their HLAs. They should have them written in their phones. They should filter their daily "yes" and "no" responses based on these items—the most critical activities that apply to their area of responsibility. Make this a reality in your organization, and I am confident you will produce the results you desire at speeds that will amaze you. And then continuing the HLA focus will continue the superior results.

Drive extraordinary results faster, and the world will reward you, whether the organization you lead is 3 people, 30, 300, or thousands. It's that simple.

HLA thinking is the silver bullet to achieving results!

Finally, please keep in touch; send me your success stories via email to info@tonyjeary.com. Call us if the time is right to engage us in helping your organization. Celebrate your successes with your team, and continue the commitment to live a life focused on HLAs.

Cheers to the RIGHT RESULTS FASTER!

Serving the best…

Tony

TAKEAWAYS - PART SIX

Acknowledgments

Thanks to my great team for helping me research, gather, write, edit, interview, and assemble this book.

Special thanks to Jim Norman, Scott Bennett, and Tawnya Austin who were the primary developers and project management of this work.

Thanks also to my editors and other content, design, and graphic contributors—Brett Duncan, Kory MacKinnon, Lori Anderson, Ross Lightle, Nonie Jobe, Alice Sullivan, Suzanne Lawing, Larry Carpenter, and Eddie Renz.

GLOSSARY OF TERMS

Blind Spots: A scotoma. An area where a person's view or viewpoint is obstructed. Failure to see things that are already in front of you. Sometimes it is a tendency to ignore something, especially because it is difficult or unpleasant.

Cascading: The well considered, consistent filtering down or across of messages throughout an organization or group (for instance, from a top executive down to his/her direct reports, down to their direct reports, and so on); messages can also cascade across to other departments, and sometimes even upward in an organization.

Clarity, Focus, Execution: The three core principles for Tony Jeary's *Strategic Acceleration* methodology.

High Leverage Activities (HLAs): The base methodology of Tony Jeary's bestselling book *Strategic Acceleration*, HLAs are efficient actions that result in the most valuable outcomes. These are the 6-8 activities that produce the most amount of results when focused on, and that you want to spend the majority of your time doing and leveraging.

Low Leverage Activities (LLAs): The things that consume your time that have the least amount of return. They are typically task-oriented in nature and become distractions to your focus.

Leverage: Use something for maximum impact; the power or ability to act or to influence people, events, decisions, etc.

MOLO (More Of, Less Of): A simple exercise to help an individual or organization identify what they need to eliminate so they can focus on what matters most; an evaluation of what should be done More Often and Less Often to ensure time is best invested on proactive, productive HLAs instead of on time-wasting, less effective tasks. Top leaders model self-reflection and continuous improvement.

Results Board: A visual representation of goals and vision that motivates you to achieve them.

Stakeholder Matrix: The matrix is a snapshot view of those people in your world who are stakeholders in your desired outcomes. Understanding what is important to them and what each wants will allow you to do things to ensure every person wins.

Strategic Acceleration: Tony Jeary's proven methodology that helps people get clear, stay focused, and efficiently execute relevant, high-value activities, thereby delivering results and success faster.

Strategic Acceleration Quotient (SAQ): An assessment to determine an individual's abilities and skills to drive results fast. Take the assessment at www.saqassessment.com.

Strategic Presence: A leader's "personal brand," lived out through actions and words, that compels others to support objectives.

Top of Mind: The thing that consumes your thinking and problems that stay in your head; your greatest concerns and/or priorities; the most important or pressing things.

ABOUT TONY JEARY

Tony Jeary is a results strategist. Many call him The RESULTS Guy™ because of this simple fact—he helps clients get the right results faster. He is a unique and powerful facilitator and subject matter expert who has advised over 1,000 clients and published over forty books. His studio process of live note taking, combined with his *Strategic Acceleration* methodology, is a secret weapon for his special clients. Tony has invested the past 25+ years developing facilitation processes and systems that allow him and his team to accelerate results, doing planning meetings in a single day, and producing results that often take days, weeks, and months in a single eight-hour session. That's a rare gift.

The world's greatest CEOs recognize the importance of thinking, strategy, and communication; and many seek Tony for all three of these. He's a gifted encourager who helps clarify visions.

The primary goal of all leaders is to enhance value and communicate their vision effectively so that their teams can execute that vision in the marketplace. Tony personally coaches presidents and CEOs of Walmart, TGI Friday's, New York Life, Firestone, Samsung, Ford, Texaco, and SAM's; even those on the Forbes richest 400 engage Tony for his advice. Tony personally helps these top leaders: define their goals; accelerate their opportunities; create, establish, and build their personal brands and careers; deliver powerful paradigm-shifting presentations; grow their leadership abilities; and accelerate the right results faster! He and/or his whole firm can be booked through his business manager. Tony Jeary International can be retained to do amazing things to support accelerated RESULTS.

What Can Tony Jeary International Do For You?

Culture Change

We change company cultures. *Strategic Acceleration* is a methodology that gets the right results faster for selected clients that have a true appetite for advancing their vision to reality quicker. Our *Strategic Acceleration* methodology is foolproof because it's not theory, academia or new. It's proven, based on real results and works every time. Please Watch the 90 second video on "Change Your Thinking, Change Your Results" at changeyourthinkingchangeyourresults.com. We get results!

Strategic Planning

Let us work with you to develop a customized strategic plan for more clarity, focus, and execution, hence more accelerated results! We develop powerful plans in a single day that take most people three days minimum and often weeks. We have a custom-built Strategic Acceleration Studio designed specifically for this offering.

Results Coaching

Having coached many of the world's top CEOs and earners, Tony understands the need for speed in today's marketplace. Benefit from 20 years of best practices from the best of the best. If you operate an organization that has millions to be made, and you're interested in sharpening your executive leadership effectiveness, let's talk.

Culture-Changing Web Trainings

Most organizations struggle with weekly meetings and poor email standards, resulting in too many meetings and too many emails, costing valuable time. Results are dramatically being hurt because of people operating in overwhelm. Tony has taken his expertise and developed simple 45-minute web trainings that can save thousands of non-productive hours for an organization and greatly impact results. Let us discuss impacting your culture. Subjects include (among others):

Email Effectiveness	Meeting Mastery
Engagement	Change Your Thinking
The Art of Results	Time Effectiveness
Influence	

KEYNOTE SPEECHES

Tony is available for unique keynote experiences that dramatically impact audiences of all sizes. Topics include *Strategic Acceleration* and *Leverage*, among others.

OTHER BOOKS BY TONY

Change Your Thinking, Change Your Results	changethinkingchangeresults.com
Strategic Acceleration	strategicacceleration.com
Business Ground Rules	businessgroundrules.com
Ultimate Health	ultimatehealth-book.com
Life Is a Series of Presentations	mrpresentation.com
How to Gain 100 Extra Minutes a Day	tonyjeary.com
Designing Your Own Life	tonyjeary.com

To discuss how we can bring value to you and your organization, email us at info@tonyjeary.com or call us at 817.430.9422.

HOW TO TAKE *LEVERAGE* TO ANOTHER LEVEL

From this book, you are aware of *High Leverage Activities*; now what are you going to do about it?

Here are three steps steps you can take immediately to put your HLAs into action.

1. CLARIFY YOUR DIRECTION

Take the 5-question online assessment and score the strength of your current approach to planning. The most successful people take their planning process very seriously. Do you? How often do you do it?

2. SIX-PART TEAM BLITZ

The *Leverage* Six-Part Team Blitz was designed by Tony Jeary International to help leaders navigate the process of multiplying both your individual results and the steps to implementing them with your leadership team and direct reports. It's a professional development tool created to help leaders increase the effectiveness of their teams by focusing on those things that have the greatest impact.

The Six-Part Team Blitz includes copies of *Leverage*, support videos, and a facilitator's guide to show you the specific steps to take to foster an HLA culture quickly and effectively as a 15-30 minute part of your regular team meetings.

3. INTENSIFY YOUR RESULTS WITH LIVE RESULTS PLANNING

Over the past 25 years, Tony Jeary and his agency members have poured into the strategic planning processes of some of the world's most profitable organizations and highest achievers. A single day in the Strategic Acceleration studio has served as a turning point for countless companies and individuals. Let us help you get RESULTS faster than you ever imagined possible.

Get all the details, and access to other
helpful resources at TonyJeary.com/Leverage.

CPSIA information can be obtained at www.ICGtesting.com
Printed in the USA
LVOW04s2020171014

409313LV00014B/157/P